MASTERY

The Art Of Living On Purpose

The Twelve Distinctions of Mastery

Michael A. Nitti, Erica Nitti Becker

BALBOA.PRESS
A DIVISION OF HAY HOUSE

Balboa Press books may be ordered through booksellers or by contacting:

Balboa Press
A Division of Hay House
1663 Liberty Drive
Bloomington, IN 47403
www.balboapress.com
844-682-1282

Because of the dynamic nature of the Internet, any web addresses or links contained in this book may have changed since publication and may no longer be valid. The views expressed in this work are solely those of the author and do not necessarily reflect the views of the publisher, and the publisher hereby disclaims any responsibility for them.

The author of this book does not dispense medical advice or prescribe the use of any technique as a form of treatment for physical, emotional, or medical problems without the advice of a physician, either directly or indirectly. The intent of the author is only to offer information of a general nature to help you in your quest for emotional and spiritual well-being. In the event you use any of the information in this book for yourself, which is your constitutional right, the author and the publisher assume no responsibility for your actions.

Any people depicted in stock imagery provided by Getty Images are models, and such images are being used for illustrative purposes only.
Certain stock imagery © Getty Images.

Print information available on the last page.

ISBN: 978-1-9822-7627-0 (sc)
ISBN: 978-1-9822-7629-4 (hc)
ISBN: 978-1-9822-7628-7 (e)

Library of Congress Control Number: 2021921852

Balboa Press rev. date: 11/30/2021

"To know thyself is the beginning of wisdom."
—Socrates

www.distinctionsofmastery.com

ENDORSEMENTS

Another life-enhancing book from the guru of living on purpose, in gratitude, with honesty, and love. Michael Nitti has outdone himself this time. Together with Erica, his daughter and magnificent disciple, they have created the manual everyone must use to achieve mastery in a life lived on purpose, in full light, with love and passion. Read the book, follow the guidance and exercises so honestly given, and watch it transform your life.

—Erika Schwartz, MD, Evolved Science, and best-selling author of *The New Hormone Solution, Don't Let Your Doctor Kill You,* and *The Intimacy Solution*

This book is a wonderful source of wisdom and inspiration, a compilation of universal truths. It can be read all at once, as an instruction manual, or dipped into for just the right bite that you need right now.

—Madeleine Homan Blanchard, chief coaching architect, The Ken Blanchard Companies

Mastery is a fantastic book that reveals why even when we're successful at what we do, we tend not to devote the same energy to what we can become. What is our purpose? Why are we here? Michael and Erica provide us with the answers to these and similar questions through their experiences and passion for helping others find their greatness.

As a professional horse racing jockey for thirty-four years, I understand the dedication and commitment it takes to remain at the top of your sport. I have won more than four thousand races worldwide, but I have also lost twenty-six thousand races. The important part is that I always learned from my losses so that I could reach my full potential.

Having worked with Michael on my personal challenges, I was

provided with the tools to learn from my "losses" elsewhere as well so that I could find success beyond the racetrack and within myself. Now, thanks to this book, you have the ability to apply these very same teachings. Live your dreams.

—Aaron Gryder, winner of the Dubai World Cup, world-renowned jockey, and public speaker

An inspiring, timeless, and riveting read for those dreams unrealized. Unlock your true potential and ignite your passion to pursue your dreams. This absolute gem of buried treasures is waiting for you to unearth and bust through your blocks into fulfilling your true soul's destiny. Amazing, timeless nuggets of wisdoms, along with powerful action steps to catapult you to where you ought to be—*not* where you thought you should be. Wow. An undeniable gateway to your dreams.

—Dawn Harlow, spiritual psychologist, Kundalini yoga master, and global speaker

When I first met Michael, I immediately identified him as one of those extraordinary individuals who embraces life without condition or complaint and does so with an infectious passion and desire, that others might share his joy and vision. Now, he and his daughter, Erica, present us with *Mastery*, the art of unlocking the endless wonderment within each of us. He combines knowledge and experience gained not in theory but from decades of changing other's lives for the better. This book is truly transformational, complete with incredible promise and possibility. Experience life through the lens of a true genius and never look back.

—David Morehouse, PhD, and author of *The Psychic Warrior: Inside the CIA's Stargate Program*

ACKNOWLEDGMENTS

"Keep away from people who try to belittle your ambitions. Small people always do that, but the really great make you feel that you, too, can become great as well."
—Mark Twain

Over the course of the dozen years or so that Erica and I have been privileged to have been associated with the same world-renowned organization, our coaching has been shaped by the very same distinctions you are about to learn over the next twelve chapters. We are blessed to have worked side by side with a host of incredible teachers, coleaders, and friends—all of whom have contributed more than they could possibly know to the writing of this book. To all of those who have shared their truth and impacted our lives so profoundly, we are eternally grateful.

Specifically, we are honored to have either met or otherwise participated in coursework with the following individuals, all of whom we consider mentors and whose dedication to serving others inspires us daily: Tony Robbins, Deepak Chopra, Wayne Dyer, Kenneth Blanchard, Jack Canfield, Madeleine Homan Blanchard, Robyn Benincasa, and Gangaji.

To my father (Erica's grandfather), Dominick Nitti, an original Navy SEAL (UDT 11), who served both his country during World War II, and his family, with honor. My mother, Vivian (RIP), Erica's mother, Mallie, as well as my daughter & Erica's sister, Amy, her brother, John, and every other member of our extended families, who are forever in our hearts and whom we love dearly.

To my wife, Julie, who I am privileged to have called my soul mate for more than thirty years, and to Erica's husband, Steve Becker, both of whom have been beyond supportive while we've been focusing on this book, and who have played key roles within the same organization for many years as well.

To those who have otherwise contributed in a major way to either mine or Erica's individual growth and development, both personal and business, specifically Tony Robbins, Sam Georges, Elaine Holland, Dr. Erika Schwartz, Cloe Madanes, Joseph McClendon III, Faith Gorski, Patty and David Morehouse, and Dawn Harlow.

To the many experts who gave us permission to include their wisdom (we are honored to collaborate). In addition to those previously mentioned, we thank Adyashanti, Sister Kimberly (on behalf of the late Macrina Wiederkehr), Dawna Markova, His Holiness Dalai Lama, Jim Rohn companies, Rumi Shahram Shiva, Billie Jean King, Auriela McCarthy, Gary Ryan Blair, Ron Potter Efron, Matt Furey (on behalf of the late Maxwell Maltz), Swami Sivananda, Paul Boese, and Sarah Ban Breathnach—as well as our editor: Mark Rickerby. Thank you all for enabling us to manifest this dream.

Finally, we acknowledge you, the reader, for your willingness to open your mind and for your intention to both discover and master your ability to live your life on purpose.

Enjoy the journey.

Dedicated to Francis "Frank" Clark
AKA "Mr. Orange"

CONTENTS

FOREWORD BY
ERICA NITTI BECKER

How much happier do you think you'd be if you didn't have to contend with all the drama? Although most of us would likely answer this question in the same way, even as we do our best to steer clear of it all, given how quick we are to react to anything we perceive as drama, we too often get sucked in by the very circumstances we're trying to avoid.

For much of my early life, I reacted to situations, mine or others, with unnecessary emotion. Whether it was words, time, or energy, I didn't feel I had a choice but to react the way that I was. And even though I believed that I was in control of what I was doing, I felt completely out of control because I didn't really know how I wanted to be seen or heard. Even if I had known, how could I have been any other way than how I was being at any given moment?

Through the following years of intense growth and transformation, I discovered the answers to this question and to many others that kept me from playing full-out. Questions like "What is wrong with me?" or "Why can't I just do what I know I need to do?"

Fortunately, I am blessed to have long ago stopped looking for answers to these types of questions. I have also stopped reacting to situations that once robbed me of my passion. Since I've also made it my career to inspire others to take control of how they are showing up, it's a privilege to let you know that you will soon be learning how to disregard your drama and override your reactions as well.

In light of all this, it's an honor to have been asked by my father to begin this journey by sharing with you how I first came to the realization that I have full control over my own psychology. That defining "aha" moment that is my foundation to living my life on purpose—simply because it's within me to do so—no matter what's being tossed in my direction.

After all, although it's totally normal to feel as though life is throwing us a steady supply of curveballs, whether we react to them or choose to live on purpose is always our choice.

As lucky as I was to grow up within listening distance of my father teaching his earliest clients about mastery, I paid very little attention to any of his teachings and a lot more attention to my own preteen drama, which seemed a lot more exciting.

However, within a week or so of my twelfth birthday—and as a result of a truly remarkable conversation I had with him—I finally *got* what he was saying. In that moment, I became instantly aware of my ability to disregard the curveballs and take full ownership of my emotions. My heart knew that this was no small epiphany because it redefined what I'd been calling drama and my ability to step beyond it. Still, as magical as our talk had been, the way in which it began wasn't at all that unusual, given that my mother—whom I had just worn down with an extra-large dose of whining—made it clear that I would be better off sharing my "problems" with my dad. And even though this wasn't the first time she had made this suggestion—or the first time I recall rolling my eyes as I set off in search of my father—I still recall feeling every bit as hopeless as we began to talk things through.

Knowing that he had overheard my talk with my mom, I noticed even more empathy in his voice than usual as he asked, "What's really going on?" And although I later realized he already knew the answer to that question, he listened intently as I blamed everyone else for everything that wasn't working for me. At which point, I fully expected him to see things my way—once he realized how unhappy I was—and fully appreciate why I was upset and immediately intervene on my behalf.

However, rather than react in any way to what I was saying, he calmly asked me two very specific questions, both of which inspired me to look beyond my emotions:

1. Do you like how you're feeling right now?
2. How would you prefer to feel instead?

Questions, which caught me completely off guard…

"What?" I responded. "Of course I don't want to feel this way, but since when is how I'm feeling up to me?"

And, although he had just exposed a limiting belief, given how calm and patient he was being—an OMG feeling swept over me in the form of an incredible epiphany. I had never even considered that I had it within me to override how I was reacting to long established emotional triggers that caused me to feel a certain way. In other words, I never knew I had personal control over feeling any way other than how I was already feeling at any given moment.

In a heartbeat, I felt like I'd been struck by a bolt of lightning. I truly got it. I actually freaking got it. Right there in the living room, chatting with my dad, I was suddenly aware of the fact that I had full autonomy over how I was showing up. In other words, I knew beyond any shadow of a doubt that *who I am* is not my feelings.

Like a stream of water exploding through a crack in a dam, I finally got what my father was saying. Although he had said the same thing to me in various ways before, I was finally willing to hear the message behind those two questions: that it's totally up to me to choose how I react to my thoughts and emotions. I suddenly became aware that I am a lot more powerful than I ever knew. All of us are. And even though all he did was simply tell me the truth, helping me finally get it and apply it was the best gift he had ever given me.

And although his gift felt intensely personal, it is also universal. It's a message he has shared with countless others for more than thirty-five years. It may have felt magical to me, but it really isn't. It is a simple but profound truth—and one that you are about to receive over the next twelve chapters.

Whether sharing his wisdom as a speaker, being interviewed on national television, or working one-on-one with clients all over the world (including business leaders, entrepreneurs, celebrities, and even other life coaches), no matter what his students intend to accomplish, it's never too long before they find themselves fully immersed in the "Twelve Distinctions of Mastery." You are on your way to discovering what's possible once you step beyond your mind and take full ownership of who you were born to be.

This book will not only allow you to ignore who you are *not,* it will inspire you to step fully into your power and make good on everything you were put here to do. That is a promise I don't make lightly, since because of that chat I had with my father when I was twelve, I not only refuse to settle for less—I refuse to ever bring less than all I've got to everything I do.

As a master coach myself for over ten years, I'm privileged to have found my own voice and employ it daily in changing the lives of thousands of my own clients, incorporating many of my father's teachings as I inspire others to find their voices as well.

Even as I refer to them as "my father's teachings," and although he truly is a master at what he does, these should in no way be construed as *his* teachings—as they are simply his way of imparting what he was privileged to "download from the universe" during his personal awakening some forty years ago.

The following twelve chapters are far more than a mere collection of thoughts and metaphors, as it is our intention that the following distinctions and teachings speak directly to that part of you (your true Self) that was both put here to become enlightened and fully intends for that to happen—which is precisely what will happen so long as you are willing to surrender to the truth that is already within you. In other words, if you can envision it, you can *be* it.

It's truly a gift for me to know that the teachings I grew up with as bedtime stories are now included here, purposefully reimagined as expressions of our intention to make them clear and insightful to you, so you can allow them to transform your experience of yourself. They are also an expression of how, armed with these truths, you will insist on showing up as the inherently whole and complete expression of humanity you were born to be. Lastly, it is my intention that everything you're about to read will inspire you personally and that every life you inspire in turn will have been made more magical by the miracle of your presence and your intention.

Happiness is for those who never negotiate with their little voice and refuse to live a single day without being inspired by who they're becoming and the difference they intend to make at every turn.

Let your transformation begin!
Erica Nitti Becker

INTRODUCTION

As a culture, we are forever being bombarded with strategies for how to live our best lives, and even though most of us have bought more books or attended more courses than we care to admit, we are often left feeling that there is even more we need to learn before we are finally set up to win.

Given how conditioned we are to be on the lookout for what's next, we tend to believe that for us to be truly happy, it's likely going to require *more* than we already have within us: more degrees, more money, a better relationship, a better body, or whatever else we believe we don't already have. Then, and only then, after we finally do achieve more and become better, we will finally have enough confidence, feel successful, know that we matter, and gosh darn it, people will truly like us.

And yet, since it's the belief that we need to become more that tends to cause us to hold back in the first place, and since this belief is tied directly to our inherent fear that we're not good enough, the only reason we keep having these thoughts is because our reactionary minds never stop doing what they were designed to do. So, no matter how often we feel like we're not enough, it's simply because our minds are doing their jobs.

Still, even though it's our nature to feel this way, the reason we tend to do so as often as we do is because who we believe we are supposed to be and who society wants us to be are in direct conflict with each other. It's a belief linked to our "if everyone else is doing it, it must be the right way" mentality, and it's the very reason why the road to "more, better, and I matter" is, by far, the most well-traveled road of all.

Since all the reasons we tend to remain glued to the path we are on are tied to our past, our purpose in writing this book is to both acquaint you with the road less traveled and to shine a light on each-and-every detour worth taking in support of creating the life of your dreams. In other words, allowing you to embrace everything you're about to learn as the missing pieces to a puzzle that you may not even know you've been waiting to solve—yet most likely have been, or you wouldn't be here.

However, given that you are here, and even if you've come to know any of this by other means, now is the time to put everything you already know on the shelf. This is the surest way to allow what you are about to discover to make its way beyond that part of you that feels it *already knows,* so to be open to what it will serve you to know at an entirely new level of knowing!

Even so, nothing is included here solely for the purpose of making you smarter (you are already smart). Instead, it will allow you to experience it in a way that will allow you to put it into practice as quickly as you can—even as your mind is imploring you not to.

It's our intention that each of the following teachings speak directly to that part of you—your subconscious, intuitive self—that is fully aware of the fact that everything you need is already within you and has been waiting for you to set it free. In other words, it's pretty much a done deal once you step into your power and refuse to listen to your mind whenever it's questioning your intention.

Still, given that the human mind's primary job is to steer us clear of trouble—which it does by questioning just about everything we do—our little voice tends to be stuck in an ongoing tug-of-war with itself, which is why we so often feel like a leaf in the wind, always wondering whether we're heading in the right direction.

However, this feeling is totally normal given that this is the same little voice that is forever pulling us in opposite directions—always at odds with itself—simultaneously imploring us to do whatever we must do in order to play it safe while wondering why we're not playing full-out in pursuit of our dreams.

Hence, the all-important questions: Which voice knows best—and which one should we listen to?

And even though neither voice really knows best, because one of them is a lot more likely to drown out the other—unless you intervene on your own behalf—listening to the *right* voice is precisely what you'll be learning to do over the next twelve chapters.

And if you happen to discover that you've become *more* as a result, consider it a bonus.

PREFACE

Although each person's path to mastery is personal, the steps we need to take and then build upon are fundamentally the same. And since they are the same, each of the following twelve chapters contains a compelling array of insights into a specific distinction of mastery and an equally compelling collection of teachings that will inspire you to apply those insights in a way that results in an immediate and profound shift in how you're showing up (as well as how you're feeling) in every moment.

In fact, this outcome is all but assured given that even random excerpts of Michael's teachings have been earning rave reviews on his social media for years and because these distinctions are also tied to the very same teachings that he and Erica draw from when working with their personal clients every single day. And, since both of them have been showing others "the way to mastery" for a combined total of more than forty years, as long as you take all that you're about to learn to heart, you have every right to expect that mastery is where you will ultimately arrive as well.

After all, insights followed by inspired action leads to growth, which, when applied consistently, leads to living on purpose—which ultimately leads to mastery.

Actually, the key to achieving this result and extracting all the value you can from this book is already in your pocket—an intention that you have every ability to achieve by finally understanding yourself and your patterns, declaring what you want, and then refusing not to have it.

However, in order to do so, you must vigilantly guard your intention because it is often undermined to the degree that you create judgments and stories about what this book will or won't do for you. And, since all of us are inclined to do this, it will serve you to ask yourself the following questions:

With regard to these judgments, what thoughts do you notice going through your mind right now? Are they like, "I already know all this / I've heard all this / I've tried all this"—or are they more like "I'm not really sure about any of this, so what's wrong with me?"

Again, since all of us tend to have similar thoughts, which ones do you recall having and how often?

No matter what thoughts you're having, in light of how your mind works, whatever you're observing right now is simply you—playing out existing patterns of how you approach specific situations—which ultimately determine whether you do or don't move forward in the face of those situations—all of which will be explained over the next twelve chapters.

Clearly, we are just getting started, so although you may not be expecting anything meaningful to show up just yet, your transformation actually began the moment you picked up this book. And because it did, we invite you to be willing to declare your intention right now, allowing your true voice to inspire you to embrace every little thing that does show up—and to play full-out from this moment on!

In other words, know that you are here for a reason, have faith, and trust that you are in the right place. And since you are in the right place, we urge you to take all the time you need to answer every question in the following chapters, to complete all the exercises, and then refuse to listen to your little voice when it tells you it's okay to skip anything at all. Then, notice if this is something you do elsewhere in your life: doing just enough to get by and then skipping the things that make it real.

Ultimately, although every insight you have is crucial, it's your answers to the questions that will help you gain clarity into what has been holding you back or preventing you from living on purpose, which is why it's just as crucial that you ultimately prove to your mind that *you* are in charge.

Remember, since inspiration can show up in a heartbeat, it will serve you well to remain fully open and read with childlike curiosity.

Teaching Framework

In support of you ultimately mastering *the art of living on purpose*, each of the following twelve chapters consists of both a high-level teaching narrative—designed to provide you with an expanded level of awareness relative to that specific distinction of mastery—and a series of individual *teachings (insights),* which are included to provide you with an even deeper level of understanding with regard to that specific distinction.

Given that each individual teaching is self-inclusive, and because repetition is the mother of understanding, we invite you to appreciate that the repetitive use of specific wording is intentional, and everything herein has been included for a reason. And because the reason is for you to attain a level of knowing that transcends a simple understanding of these teachings, we also invite you to allow what you are about to experience to inspire you to become a *master* of this content rather than someone who simply understands it.

> "Before we can learn, we need to learn how to learn, and
> before we can learn how to learn, we need to unlearn."
> —Sufi aphorism

SECTION I

Awareness and Self-Realization

Waking up! Becoming aware of who is actually running your life each day. By the end of this section, you will know specifically who is in charge of you!

I. Awareness; Who you truly are has very little to do with who you think you are

II. Intention and Reaction; Taking full control of your life in Every Moment

III. You are not your Mind; Your ego is an imposter, pretending to be you

Section I Exercises: Turning Awareness into Action
Living in alignment with "the truth." Learning to say no to your "little voice." How to step into your power instead of allowing your survival mind to run the show.

CHAPTER 1

Awareness

Who you truly are has very little to do with who you think you are

How aware are you of your own consciousness?

If you're not sure, ask yourself these questions: What is behind how you're showing up every day? How do you intend to show up from now on?

"One can have no smaller or greater mastery than mastery of oneself."
—Leonardo da Vinci

It's been said that the truth shall set you free. Even so, mastery has very little to do with simply *knowing* the truth; it's about *living* it.

In every moment, we are either showing up in alignment with who we truly are—or we're not. And no matter what our circumstances are, it's fully within our control to interact with everyone in our lives from an intentional, loving, and beautiful state—in which we are forever compassionate, with love and gratitude in our hearts, and in perfect alignment with flow energy and the greater good—simply because it's our intention to do so.

In other words, it's always up to you whether you're choosing to live *on purpose* or choosing not to.

Even so—and although very few of us ever perceive it as a choice—whenever you're allowing your ego to run the show, it's because you have unwittingly surrendered to your survival mind and are, by default, living *in reaction* to whatever it's screaming in your ear rather than in alignment with your vision and your intention.

Despite all the screaming, it's completely within your power to override your reactive mind and intentionally show up in a resourceful state—both because you can, and because you're choosing to do so.

Actually, what most of us have come to know as higher consciousness is simply the awareness that you own the ability to override your biology (your survival mind) and because you know that there is no reason not to—especially once you're living in alignment with the truth rather than in reaction to your instincts and history, including all that you've had to overcome and all your limiting beliefs.

Ultimately, no matter what you have been conditioned to believe, who you truly are is what's flowing *through* you, and not the entity through which it flows. The "entity" being your physical body and intellect, which your mind is hoping you will never stop believing is you.

Mastery, therefore, is for those who are living in full alignment with *what's so* and who refuse to bring anything less than their full intention to every little thing they are committed to making a reality.

In support of which, I invite you to allow the following teachings to shine a light on what's possible once you do.

Namaste.

Chapter 1 Teachings

1.1

Knowledge is the key to unlocking the door to your dreams. Wisdom is knowing which door. And yet, if you fail to step boldly beyond whichever door you choose, your accomplishments will be random at best. In fact, success has little to do with what you *know* and everything to do with what you *do* with what you know.

When it comes to living the life of your dreams, once you find your door, never let anything stop you from knocking that sucker down!

> "Whatever you can do or dream you can, begin it.
> Boldness has genius, power and magic in it."
> —Johann Wolfgang von Goethe

Intention isn't the absence of fear; it is the energy that allows you to override your mind when it's screaming at you not to. Results are for those who are quick to honor their courage more than their fear and who are just as quick to ignore the screaming.

1.2

As human beings, although we all get upset or feel sad at times, it's fully within each of us to simply have these feelings without our feelings having us. Once you accept that your feelings have no inherent meaning, you will be empowered to embrace them for what they are, which is simply proof that you are human.

Higher consciousness is a function of allowing for your emotions rather than buying into them, which is why it will serve you to honor your intention more than how you feel—and what will serve you even more is to never stop doing so.

> "The key to growth is the introduction of
> higher dimensions of consciousness."
> —Lao Tzu

Since your random thoughts are essentially meaningless, it will serve you to simply ignore them. Whether you allow your life to be shaped by something meaningful or meaningless is always up to you. Shape wisely.

1.3

Contrary to popular belief, higher consciousness has very little to do with becoming something you are not; it's about stepping beyond whatever's stopping you from showing up as who you already are.

Mastery is for those who are quick to embrace this truth and who refuse to allow anything to get in the way of expressing their magnificence as fully as possible into the universe.

Living the life of your dreams is never about finding what's missing or fixing what's broken. There is nothing missing, and you're not broken. I invite you to begin there.

> "I have come to bring out the beauty you never knew
> you had and lift you up like a prayer to the sky."
> —Rumi

Ego is an imposter that is pretending to be you. Once you replace worrying about *what* you are with showing up as *who* you are, love will show the imposter the door.

1.4

No matter the circumstances we were born into, we are inherently whole and complete just as we are. Therefore, if ever you're not achieving everything you feel you deserve, it's a lack of vision and inspired action that's holding you back—not the fact that you don't have what it takes.

In fact, whether you choose to believe it or not, you were born with what it takes.

Once you step willingly into the truth and start bringing all you've got to everything you do, the universe will just as willingly shine a light on your path.

> "Find out where joy resides and give it a voice far beyond
> singing. For to miss the joy is to miss all."
> —Robert Louis Stevenson

You are the light, you simply forgot. You are the power, yet sometimes you're scared. Although most of us tend to believe that suffering is a result of circumstances beyond our control, suffering is really a function of withholding your light and your power. Once you say *no* to withholding, joy will say *yes* to you.

1.5

If you allow yourself to observe what's so, you'll realize that there is no inherent meaning in anything at all. Therefore, the underlying story you've been telling yourself about your life is purely fiction.

Even so, there's no use in blaming yourself for buying into your own story, since the only reason you created it in the first place was because your ego compelled you to do so, in order to make amends for your otherwise less than remarkable existence.

Mastery, therefore, is for those who are just as quick to leave their mind's story behind as they are to begin writing one of their own.

"You never change things by fighting the existing reality. To change something, build a new model that makes the old model obsolete."
—Buckminster Fuller

In every moment, we have total control over what we're present to and the meaning we attach to it. Any perceived exception to this truth is an illusion. Mastery is for those who have chosen to align with the truth and not the illusion.

1.6

Freedom is a function of accepting what is.

Happiness is shifting your focus from looking for what's missing to appreciating what's present.

Success is desiring more and refusing not to have it.

Mastery is knowing that life is a game and being grateful for every opportunity to play.

Bliss is igniting the fire in your heart and sharing your love and your light with the universe.

If you want to wake up on fire, *be* the flame.

"If a problem has a solution, we must work to find it; if it does not, we need not waste time thinking about it".
—Dalai Lama

Consciousness is for those who have checked their egos at the door to the truth. Enlightenment is for those with the courage to leave it there.

1.7

At the very core of our existence burns a fire and a passion, that even as it renders us personally unstoppable, is where all of us are inherently connected, as one.

And yet, within the shadow of this fire lives an imposter—otherwise known as *ego*—that is forever causing us to question both the validity of our passion and our oneness with Source. Unfortunately, when you give in to your ego, you not only give up your connection to *that* which is flowing through all of us, you are letting the universe know that you've chosen to go it alone.

I encourage you to rethink going it alone.

> "For a man to conquer himself is the first and noblest of all victories."
> —Plato

Mastery is for those who are willing to question everything they think, including where they are thinking it from. Once you get a glimpse of what's really going on, there's no turning back.

1.8

Although intention and love flow naturally, whether you *go with the flow* or resist it is always up to you. At the end of the day, being of service (living on purpose and in support of the greater good) is not only our highest calling, but the underlying essence of flow.

Conversely, giving in to your ego (living in reaction) is the very source of our resistance to flow. If your intention is to override your ego, the only way to do so is to shift your focus from what's in it for you to what's in it for others. Once you do, you'll soon discover what's in it for you.

"When you allow source energy to flow through your heart, your heart, soul, and mind exude radiance. As you are overflowing with the power of grace, your greatest rewards for existence, are to give the gifts of grace to all who cross your sacred path. Nothing more can fulfill your soul's mission than to be a loving force for the light."

—Nancy Penttila Lemire

Happiness is for those who replace waking up worrying about what they're going to get with waking up already knowing what they're going to give.

1.9

As a result of our conditioning, we are inclined to believe that if we simply stay our course along a path of higher learning, we will ultimately attain nirvana. However, enlightenment has nothing to do with searching for something beyond yourself; it is about unleashing what's already within you.

For the most part, it's our very seeking the divine that gives rise to our separation from it, for why else would any of us need to seek anything that's already present?

In fact, the truth is forever flowing through each of us, so the only thing preventing you from experiencing yourself as the enlightened being you truly are, is the belief that you are not.

Once you give up the search for who you already have it within you to be, you'll be inspired to kick the imposter to the curb.

"The one who was always in my thoughts, for whom I've searched so long, has come to me with open arms, laying flowers on my path."
—Rumi

If ever you're feeling lost, only by being willing to step beyond your lost-ness will you find your way—which lies just beyond the illusion that you've lost your way.

1.10

You and I are pure love waiting to happen. And yet, the illusion that we are separate from one another not only prolongs the wait it allows the ego to justify our need to win at the expense of others.

Once you embrace the fact that all of us are inherently connected, as one, you will naturally and intuitively replace your ego's perception that you are simply *in* the world with a knowing in your heart that you *are* the world. In every moment, who you truly are is the energy flowing through you, not the entity through which it flows.

> "The ultimate value of life depends upon awareness, and the power of contemplation, rather than upon mere survival."
> —Aristotle

Consciousness is a function of accessing the love that's already flowing through you and allowing yourself to be used by *that* rather than by your ego. Once you call off the search for who you are, you'll be able to see that you already are who you've been searching for. I invite you to be that.

1.11

Given how often we tend to lament anything we've yet to attain or experience, we are just as likely to believe that *true* happiness exists solely outside the realm of our everyday existence. And yet, only by letting go of the belief your ability to be truly happy lives somewhere beyond the mundaneness of how we normally show up will you be able to experience the full measure of your aliveness and passion—whether you are already engaged in checking items off your *bucket list,* or simply spending time at home with your family.

In fact, it's our conditioning and "fear of missing out" that prevents us from extracting all the joy we can out of our daily activities—not the routineness of what we're doing or whether it meets our standards for what it takes to light us up.

Whether you're aware of it or not, *you* are the source of your own light, but you must be willing to access the magic that's already within you in support of setting it free.

"It is not in the stars to hold our destiny, but in ourselves."
—William Shakespeare

Mastery is for those with the wisdom to bring joyfulness along for the ride rather than hoping it shows up once they get where they're going.

1.12

For the most part, we have been socially conditioned to believe that our only options in life are one way or the other. However, by simply acknowledging this conditioning and remaining open to seeing things as they truly are, you'll finally be granted access to options that were previously obscured by the belief that you have no other options.

In fact, the only situations in life where things tend to be governed by the constraints of *either/or* are when we choose to pay attention to our conditioning rather than to what's *really* going on.

Freedom is for those who refuse to pay any attention at all to their conditioning.

"Life is a balance of holding on and letting go."
—Rumi

There are many things in life that will grab your attention, but only a few will speak to your soul. Follow the ones that speak to your soul.

1.13

Everything you are putting into the universe today will either serve you or haunt you tomorrow.

In every moment, the way in which you are showing up and how you treat others is the key to unlocking whichever box of karma with your name on it that you find down the road.

Therefore, only by being fully conscious of what you're leaving in your wake as you're creating it will you be inclined to find the box with all the goodies.

Joyfulness is for those who bring so much love and compassion along for the ride that they can't help but shine their light as brightly as they can on everyone and everything.

> "Man stands in his own shadow and wonders why it's dark."
> —Zen proverb

Attempting to control the actions of others will never serve you. Mastery is for those who are fully aware of how they are "being" in every moment, who make requests rather than demands, and who consistently show up as deserving rather than entitled. Once you commit to showing up this way, everything you've ever wanted will begin flowing in your direction.

1.14

If you've ever been humbled by a fall from grace and thought about it afterward, you probably realized that there was a point just before your fall where you began making it more about *you* than about your intention to contribute beyond yourself.

Although you certainly deserve to benefit from your endeavors, it will serve you to consider that your fall was the universe's way of reminding you that it's not solely about you.

For that reason, I invite you to take the hint, realign with your purpose (rather than with your ego), and put yourself back out there with an intention to make the incredible difference you were born to make.

> "As flies are to wanton boys, are we to the
> gods. They kill us for their sport."
> —William Shakespeare, *King Lear*

Given that what's showing up in your universe is simply a reflection of what you're sending it, things can only go off track if you are. Humility is a function of thinking more about what you're putting out there than about what *out there* thinks about you.

1.15

Life is fired at us point-blank. Yet only by embracing your inherent intuitiveness will you become disciplined enough to say *no* to anything that doesn't serve you and *yes* to everything that does.
Mastery is for those who are quick to celebrate life as the treasure hunt that it is and even quicker to run from anything that might distract them from seeing the treasure in every little thing.
In every moment, whether you're hunting for treasure or drama is totally up to you.
Hunt wisely.

> "You are allowed to be both a masterpiece and
> work in progress at the same time."
> —Unknown

If you sit around waiting for what you want to find you, the only thing you'll discover is that it didn't find you while you were sitting around waiting. Unless and until you give up the wait, you'll likely be waiting forever.

1.16

As a function of being human, you and I are inclined to not only perceive ourselves as specific points of view (from which we interpret everything in our lives as reality), we tend to reject anything that doesn't seem to fit. In other words, because the ego is threatened by conflicting points of view, it compels us to promote and defend our personal points of view as *correct* while dismissing all others.

Even so, what we tend to perceive as reality only shows up this way because the culture has conditioned us to believe what we perceive.

For instance, a fish has no clue that it's swimming in water because from its perspective, water is all there is—which is why flying fish are so quick to see the truth once they take their very first leap into the unknown.

Only by being willing to call into question all your strongly held perceptions and beliefs will you be able to experience yourself as the limitless and enlightened being you truly are.

Mastery is for those who are willing to take the leap.

> "If the doors of perception were cleansed, everything
> would appear to man as it is, infinite."
> —William Blake

> "When you're aware, the thoughts you frequent and the
> words you choose are authentic and potent. With awareness
> you can consciously create your dream life."
> —Niurka

The first step toward discovering who you truly are is to accept that you've been hypnotized into believing who you are not.

Chapter 1 Key Concept

You have been withholding the part of you that is your true self—the part of you that you have been hypnotized into believing that it can only be found outside yourself.

> "The truth is that you already are what you are seeking."
> —Adyashanti

CHAPTER 2

Intention and Reaction

Taking Full Control of Your Life in Every Moment

How aware are you of your inclination to fall into reaction?

What tends to set you off (certain people, specific situations, life circumstances, or your own perceptions) more than anything else? Why is that?

> "He who controls others may be powerful, yet he
> who has mastered himself is mightier."
> —Lao Tzu

Mastery is for those who replace waking up in reaction to how they're feeling with waking up already knowing how they're going to show up.

Unless you skipped the first chapter, you are likely already on board with the fact that you are either living in alignment with who you truly are—on purpose—or paying way too much attention to whatever your survival mind has to say.

Once you accept that you are in control of your own psychology, you'll immediately realize that you are not your little voice—so you'll also know that there's no reason to listen to anything it's telling you. In fact, by simply honoring your intention more than your biology, you will know that it's forever within your power to override your reactive mind—even when it's begging you not to.

No matter how uncertain we may feel at times, life is basically a process of dancing as best we can with every little thing flowing in our direction. And although your mind will forever question the quality of your dancing, your ability to both dance *on purpose* and as brilliantly as possible is clearly an intention over which all of us have complete control—even though it typically doesn't feel this way.

Clearly, we truly are in charge, but the reason it doesn't always feel that way is because our survival mind is always in the background, looking for situations that it perceives as threats. And since looking for these threats is its job, it's inclined to find them at every turn. At which point, it's equally inclined to take immediate control of everything you say and do, all to ensure that you survive whatever's going on and that your ego doesn't take a hit. That is, until your survival mind perceives yet another threat, which inspires your ego to raise yet another red flag, prompting the entire process to play out again.

Until you're willing to take full ownership of this dynamic—which you have likely come to know as fight-or-flight mode—and are equally willing to take back control from your survival (instinctual) mind, it will not only continue to steer you where *it* wants to go (on behalf of your ego), there's also a pretty good chance that you'll continue to miss out on all the love and joy that's waiting for you on the other side of your fears.

But even as you are able to observe this survival dynamic going on in the background, there is still one more thing you need to know in order to override your fight-or-flight programming and take full control of your own psychology—and that is to notice that no matter how we feel about whatever's going on around us, there are actually only two ways that we ever show up in response to it. And even though we tend to experience all kinds of thoughts and feelings as life unfolds, there are still only two ways (either one way or the other) that we're inclined to show up in any given moment. In fact, as a result of this either/or dynamic, no matter how you may be feeling in that moment, you are either showing up in the first (and most powerful) of these two ways—on purpose—or you're not. And when you're not, it's because you have fallen prey to the second way of showing up, which is known as *reaction*.

Reaction is tied directly to your fight-or-flight wiring, and is, in fact, your default way of showing up—so unless you're showing up in a fully intentional state, you are literally wired to show up *in reaction* to what your survival mind is whispering in your ear. And what it's usually whispering about is how you should rethink doing anything that might result in your falling short or otherwise appearing foolish.

For this reason, I invite you to observe how this dynamic is playing out in your own life and how critical it is to take full ownership of your ability to immediately intervene on your own behalf.

Whenever you catch yourself showing up in anything other than an intentional state—though it may very well be that there really is something truly dangerous going on at that moment—it's more often the result of your mind reacting in a *preemptive way* to what it perceives as your chances of something not going your way in general. This is often merely the result of being distracted by your underlying fears and limiting beliefs *or* being reminded of something that didn't go well in the past.

In other words, no matter where you are or what you're committed to, you are either showing up *on purpose* or your survival mind has taken over and you're living *in reaction* to something that you're either concerned about in that very moment or you're thinking about a negative experience you had previously.

Fortunately, once you fully understand the inner workings of your survival mind, no matter what it is you're reacting to, your inherent ability to override it will begin to show up the very moment you realize you're in reaction.

As you can imagine, this is no small ability, given that we have *zero* control over how often we fall into a reactive state. And although you have *full* control over how long you allow yourself to stay there, until you fully embrace *the reasons* why you fall into reaction—and the reasons behind the reasons—you'll likely continue to find it a struggle to shift yourself back into *intention*.

In fact, until you fully understand *why* you fall into reaction when you do, your chances of overriding your survival mind and shifting back into your power are random at best. However, once you're willing to take full ownership of the two reasons that cause you to get sucked into reaction so often, you will know that you have absolute autonomy over your reactive mind!

Of course, since you may not be feeling this autonomy just yet, this is precisely what we're about to explore next. In support of which, I invite you to allow the following teachings to inspire you to begin to take ownership of *who you truly are.*

Chapter 2 Teachings

2.1

As human beings, we have very little control over the ebb and flow of our emotions. However, we have total control over how quickly we're able to override our reactionary responses to those emotions, which is a function of both interrupting our own patterns and stepping fully into our power. Once you accept that it's totally normal for us to fall into reaction when we do—in response to any perceived threats to our ego—you'll be empowered to redirect your focus and your physiology back into alignment with the fully intentional superhero you were born to be.

No matter what life throws your way, it's forever within your power to override your reactionary mind by willfully showing up, *on purpose*, while ignoring the ebb and flow.

All the joy in the world is for those who do.

> "People are always blaming their circumstances for what they are.
> I don't believe in circumstances. The people who get on in the
> world are the people who get up and look for the circumstances
> they want and, if they can't find them, make them."
> —George Bernard Shaw

Wisdom is for those who refuse to engage with others when they're angry or make any decisions when they're sad. Even though you may not always feel like it, you are the author of your life. Mastery, therefore, is for those who are unwilling to create anything other than a masterpiece.

2.2

Since none of us would ever intend to be unhappy on purpose, unhappiness can only show up when we stop intending to be happy. In other words, unhappiness is simply the lack of an ongoing intention to show up in a beautiful state, which, paradoxically, is where we end up by default when we're living in reaction to not being happy.

Although it's totally normal for us to fall into reaction when we do, it's fully within our power to embrace the fact that nothing can make us stay there. In fact, whether or not you believe that you have full control over your own psychology, all of us were born with the ability to shift back into an intentional state no matter how often we fall prey to reaction.

Still, and even though you are in charge of whatever you're bringing to the party at any given moment, mastery is never a function of simply *knowing* that you are in charge, it's a function of *showing up* like you are in charge.

> "Knowing others is intelligence. Knowing yourself is true wisdom.
> Mastering others is strength. Mastering yourself is power."
> —Lao Tzu

Given that you would never choose to be upset, whenever you're unhappy for any reason, it's simply because you've fallen into reaction. At that point, in order to avoid regretting whatever you say next, wisdom is for those who shift back into intention before saying anything at all.

2.3

Fortunately, within the heartbeat that separates your mind's perception of a threat from your inclination to react lives the option of either letting your ego do your talking or showing up in alignment with your intentional self. The tools available to the ego are justification, blame, avoidance, domination, and the need to be right. The tools available to the Self are love, compassion, truth, honor, gratitude, and courage.

In every moment, it's totally up to you which toolbox you bring to the party, but if your intention is to show up as the incredible shining star you were born to be, I invite you to bring the box with the love.

"Between stimulus and response, there is a space. In that
space lies our freedom and power to choose our response.
In our response lies our growth and freedom."
—Viktor Frankl

Be conscious of what you're leaving in your wake as you're creating it, and you'll be rewarded with a fuller appreciation of the now and a future in which your happy memories far outnumber your regrets.

2.4

Whenever we fall into reaction—living at the effect of the survival mind and the ego—the winds of change are bound to blow us off course. However, once you intentionally step back into your power and choose to live on purpose—while knowing that it's fully up to you to adjust your own sails—you'll discover that life's a breeze.

"The first to apologize is the bravest.
The first to forgive is the strongest.
The first to forget is the happiest."
—Unknown

Are you living life—or is it living you? In every moment, we are either living in alignment with our vision and our purpose or allowing our survival mind to lead us around by the nose. By simply refusing to be the leaf, and choosing instead to be the wind, you'll realize that who's really in charge is *you*.

2.5

Fear is a function of our survival instinct, which means we are literally programmed to believe that it's better to be safe than sorry. Even so, although our instincts are inclined to steer us toward the path of least resistance, each of us has the desire to dream bigger dreams and the ability to override our instincts in favor of making those dreams come true. In other words, no matter what your little voice is whispering in your ear, whether you choose to dance with your passion or surrender to your instincts is always up to you.

"There is a morning inside you waiting to burst into Light."
—Rumi

Whenever you're feeling fearful, if you continue to focus on what you're afraid of, you'll lose sight of who you truly are. Happiness is for those who spend more time focusing on what's possible rather than on worrying about what isn't.

2.6

Anger, born of reaction, has the ability to do as much damage in less time than a tornado winding its way through a trailer park. That being the case, if ever you're feeling angry, it will serve you to step beyond your inclination to go off on others with an intention to resolve things more gracefully. To do so, you must first be willing to override your reactionary energy with an intention to make things right (versus making others wrong).
No matter how quickly you're able to get someone's attention when you yell, there is never a question to which anger is the best possible answer. Intention, on the other hand, always saves the day.

"Anger is an acid that can do more harm to the vessel in which
it is stored than to anything on which it is poured."
—Mark Twain

Allowing your voice to serve as a loudspeaker for your ego or as a messenger of your heart is always up to you. Although it will surely serve you to speak your truth, it will serve you even more to let love do your talking.

2.7

Given our inherent fear of not being good enough, most of us spend so much time trying to avoid looking like an ass, that we rarely experience what it's like to put ours on the line.

Consequently, unless you're willing to step beyond your fear of being judged, all that you'll ever accomplish will be shaped by what you already feel you can do without appearing foolish.

When you disavow your intention by avoiding something you know must be done, you rob yourself of your aliveness and your effectiveness as well. Mastery, therefore, is for those who not only refuse to surrender to their reactive mind, they honor their courage more than their fear by intentionally putting an end to the thievery.

> "Your purpose in life is to find your purpose and
> to give your whole heart and soul to it."
> —Buddha

Courage is never about not being afraid of whatever you're afraid of; it's about being willing to override your mind when it's pleading with you not to.

2.8

For the most part, higher consciousness is a function of paying closer attention to your mouth. When dieting, it's important to monitor what goes into it. In a relationship, it's important to monitor what comes out. When you do open it, it will serve you to do so intentionally; if you ever feel the need to criticize anyone, it will serve you even more to keep it closed. And when it is closed, teach it to smile.

Once you override your mind and take full ownership of your mouth, you'll realize that the only thing flowing out of it is love.

> "Better to remain silent and be thought a fool than
> to open your mouth and remove all doubt."
> —Abraham Lincoln

Since you would never say anything hurtful to anyone on purpose, if you catch yourself doing so, it's because you're listening to whatever your reactionary mind is whispering in your ear. Wisdom is for those who have replaced listening to their minds with putting their hearts in charge of their mouths.

2.9

Although patience is a virtue, putting off doing what you know must be done has nothing to do with patience. Rather, patience is the ability to embrace delayed gratification only after you are actively engaged in the pursuit of what you desire. In fact, putting off the pursuit is a function of fear. So, when focusing on an outcome, the only thing it will serve you to put on the back burner is fear itself.

Mastery, therefore, is for those with the wisdom to put their fears on hold and not their intentions.

> "Let yourself be silently drawn by the strange pull of
> what you really love. It will not lead you astray."
> —Rumi

> "To attain mastery, one must not just know the
> path, one must actually live the path."
> —Steve A. Becker

When you are living in reaction (allowing your ego and your survival instinct to run the show), the winds of change are bound to blow you off course. When you are living on purpose (intentional, yet willing to adjust your sails), life's a breeze…

2.10

In the grand scheme of things, it's never about what you're looking at; it's about what you see. And yet, what we're inclined to see is what we expect to see, which tends to be shaped by what we've seen before.

In fact, how we react in the moment tends to mirror how we've reacted in the past, which is why most of us are living lives that are little more than regurgitated versions of our history.

To break free of this trap, it's critical that you bring your full presence and intention to everything you do and own it as a gift to both yourself and others. Remember, you are not only the creator of your own experience; you are the author of your tomorrow.

In celebration of this truth, I invite you to spend the rest of your life writing a masterpiece.

> "If you look into your heart, and you find nothing wrong there, what is there to worry about? What is there to fear?"
> —Confucius

Are you living life or is it living you? No matter your circumstances, you are either showing up as the wind beneath your own wings or living at the whim of whatever's blowing you around in the moment. Mastery is for those who both refuse to be the dust and have every intention of *being* the wind!

2.11

If ever you feel you've thought of everything yet still haven't resolved a specific situation, it's because it's never about what you're thinking; it's about *where* you're thinking from.

In fact, if the answer existed somewhere within the realm of what you already know, you'd have figured it out by now.

Unfortunately, since we do most of our thinking from within the confines of our reactionary minds, we're inclined to remain stuck where we are.

Mastery, therefore, is for those who are both thinking from beyond the confines and doing all of their thinking on purpose.

> "I don't fix problems, I fix my thinking. Then problems fix themselves."
> —Louise Hay

In order to resolve anything you're not happy with, if you truly want things to turn out as you'd like them to be, you must first be willing to see them as they actually are.

2.12

Setbacks are only temporary unless we declare them to be failures. In other words, whether you allow your mistakes to live as proof that you're not good enough or as lessons is totally up to you. In fact, whenever we are feeling down, it's never because of whatever went wrong; it's because we are *lamenting* what went wrong. Obviously, it's impossible to live a life that's free of things going wrong, but it's totally possible to live a life that's free of lamenting them.

Lamenting serves no purpose other than to make us feel like crap. Unless you enjoy feeling like crap, I invite you to give up lamenting.

"What a wonderful life I've had. I only wish that I'd realized it sooner."
—Collette

As the author of your life, it's always up to you as to whether you're collecting lemons or lessons. In every moment, you are fully in charge of whether you're simply having a bad day or if your bad day is having you. Choose wisely.

Chapter 2 Key Concept

Happiness is an intention. You must live each day believing that how you're feeling is your responsibility—and then choose to show up that way!

"Happiness is not by chance, but by choice."
—Jim Rohn

CHAPTER 3

You Are Not Your Mind

Your ego is an imposter, pretending to be you

Who is in charge of you right now? You—or your ego? What needs to change?

> "You have power over your mind, not outside events.
> Realize this, and you will find strength."
> —Marcus Aurelius

Mastery is for those with the wisdom to replace their concerns about who they are *not* with an intention to show up as who they've always had it within them to be. And yet, since our survival mind has no inclination at all to support us in pulling this off, we tend to spend most of our time living *in reaction* to our doubts and fears, rather than honoring our vision and purpose.

And although it's fully within our power to override our instincts, given that our survival mind is forever pleading with us not to, we're inclined to ask ourselves the following questions whenever we catch ourselves in reaction:

- Why is it that we slip into reaction as often as we do?
- Once we're in reaction, why do we tend to remain there for as long as we do?

Thanks to our biology, there are two specific reasons why all of us fall into reaction so often, and even though being fully aware of these reasons will leave you fully set up to win, unless you commit to living from what you know, the only thing you'll likely get is *smarter*.

Still, and even though smarter is a good thing, only by taking full ownership of these two reasons—while also *overriding* them—will you ultimately know all you need to know in support of living intentionally and on purpose, as well as anything else you intend to master.

Therefore, and in support of you attaining mastery, you must begin with all that you learned in the first two chapters:

- All of us operate from a reactive state of mind more often than not.
- Although we sometimes find our way back into intention (after all, even a blind squirrel finds an acorn every now and then), our ability to do so is clearly random at best; leaving us with no understanding at all of what we did or how we did it.
- Without that awareness, you have very little chance of doing it often enough to make a difference.

By staying the course and embracing everything you're about to learn, by the end of this chapter, you will know exactly how you found your way back—and you'll know exactly what you overcame so that you can continue to do so *forever*.

Again, there have been times in the past when you showed up *on purpose*. And since what you clearly overcame back then was your mind imploring you not to, it's obviously within your power to keep doing so. However, since your mind would prefer that you simply let *it* run the show, what's clearly happening when you step beyond your mind and shift from reaction to intention is that, in that moment, you are consciously choosing to disregard the two reasons that would otherwise cause you to remain in reaction.

You see, even when you have overridden your mind and found your way into intention, whenever you were able to do so, you literally pulled it off without even knowing what these two reasons were. In other words, although you may have *showed up* as that blind squirrel, more often than not, you simply got lucky.

However, since *getting lucky* isn't something you can count on, it will serve you to both give up relying on your chances of showing up as the squirrel and embrace everything you're about to learn about the two reasons. You see, by simply taking ownership of your biological programming and appreciating how much your "squirrel-ness" has impacted your psychology, you'll find that instead of making yourself wrong for falling into reaction, you'll be inspired to shift yourself back into intention, simply because its within you to do so.

And yet, until you're willing to accept that it's totally normal to fall into reaction when you do, your chances of shifting out of it are slim, at best—especially if you have no clue as to why it's even happening.

Therefore, in support of you enhancing your chances, while also cutting right to the chase, it will further serve you to know that even though the two reasons we fall into reaction are tied directly to our biology, the *primary* reason we react as often as we do is simply because we are *animals.* And since we are, not only are we forever on the lookout for anything we perceive as a threat, "reaction" is *always* our first response!

After all, animals are driven by biology and history. Not intellect.

Of course, you've always known that you're an animal, but when was the last time that you—or anyone else you know—literally woke up thinking, *Gee, I wonder how my survival instinct is gonna take me through the day?* Never, right? And yet, since survival is the primary focus and ultimate purpose of every animal's mind, it's literally impossible to separate ourselves from our fight-or-flight biology. And, since all of us have grown so accustomed to living in reaction to our instincts, we're inclined to accept *reaction* as "just the way things are."

What's more, unless you replace *acceptance* with taking ownership of your instincts, your instincts will continue to take ownership of you!

Just like every other animal on the planet, human beings react to just about everything our minds perceive as a threat. In fact, whenever an animal in the wild hears a noise but doesn't know what it is, it instantly freezes up in response to its survival mind wondering, *What the hell was that?* And then, unless it knows the source of whatever it hears next, *it's outta there!*

Even so, whether "outta there" is something it does by way of running, burrowing into the ground, or quickly climbing a tree, what it *doesn't* do is stick around to find out what made that noise.

And yet, even when an animal does choose *outta there* over sticking around, it rarely gets very far before noticing that it's not being chased by anything dangerous—often realizing instead that what it had perceived as a threat was nothing more than a couple of rabbits playing in some leaves.

Still, in the wake of any such false alarm, animals have no issue at all with reacting like they do. And although they are just fine with allowing their instincts to steer them clear of anything that may want to have them for lunch, this dynamic plays out much differently with human beings.

Specifically, even though your mind will surely take you out of the way of a speeding bus if it must, it typically spends most of its time reacting to perceived threats to your *ego,* imploring you to avoid them at all costs.

As a result, whenever your mind detects even the slightest possibility that you might lose (or that someone else might win) or that you might be wrong (and that somebody else might be right) or that you are about to be dominated by anyone else in any way, it will instantly prompt you to react in order to survive what it just perceived as a threat to your ego—just as if you were about to get hit by that bus.

In fact, within a heartbeat of your mind perceiving even the tiniest threat, it will instantly compel you to do whatever it takes for you to avoid that threat and survive, which is why you are always so quick to slip into reaction when anyone doubts you or when you otherwise feel like you're being diminished in any way.

Which is why, the fact that we are animals with a survival instinct is the first of the two reasons why we tend to spend so much of our time in reaction. Which is also why it's critical for us to forgive ourselves for doing so, which will help us shift back into intention and to show up as the incredible force for good that we truly are.

Now that you're aware that the first reason we fall into reaction is tied to the fact that we are literally wired to do so, the very fact that we're "wired to do so" is what causes us to fall even deeper into reaction! And, when we do, since the fact that we tend to fall deeper into reaction causes us to feel like we're not good enough, "feeling like we're not good enough" is the *second reason* we fall into reaction as often as we do!

What's more, since we tend to feel like we're not good enough every time we fall into reaction, we're inclined to react to our own reactions, which pretty much seals the deal. Worse yet, unless and until we intentionally interrupt this pattern, *reaction* is where we're likely to stay.

Unfortunately, even as we're doing our best to make something magical happen, our survival mind is always looking for proof that we don't have what it takes to do so. As a result, we are never more than a single perceived threat away from being reminded that we're not good enough—and in reaction to that thought—getting sucked even deeper into reaction.

After all, even if you don't feel like you're looking for proof, your mind is still doing so on your behalf. So, unless you intentionally override your mind and call off the search, it will keep searching until it finds what it's looking for, which is any evidence that you're not good enough! Worse yet, it won't give up until it finds it.

Think about it, if you tell a four-year-old that there's a monster in his closet, what's he going to be looking for every time he opens the closet door? That's right, a monster—because his mind is looking for proof that it's true.

Thanks to our inherent fear of not being good enough, your mind has literally been collecting proof that it's true your entire life. And even though everything it's been collecting is nothing other than proof that you are *human,* your mind has been storing it all as proof that you're not good enough!

After every new piece of proof is added to your collection, two things happen—you react to how poorly you feel about the content of your *collection*, and you remain on the lookout for even more proof, which perpetuates the cycle. And since we all make mistakes, your mind is guaranteed to find all the proof it's looking for more often as not, and unless you intervene on your own behalf, it's going to keep searching, continuing to hold onto *every* piece of proof it finds… forever!

Therefore, it's imperative that you stop looking for proof to add to your collection, or even say goodbye to your collection altogether. And yet, even as you refuse to listen to your mind moving forward, it will continue to look for proof that you're a threat to your own survival—right up until you check out —which is why it's just as critical that you always say *no* to your little voice when it pleads with you to let *it* run the show.

As you can imagine, since it's fully vested in you playing small, your mind isn't at all happy with the fact that you now know everything you do about the two reasons. In fact, it's been hoping that you would have made it all the way until it no longer matters without ever learning about any of these truths.

What's more, it's likely screaming in your ear right now, trying to convince you that you would be crazy to pay any attention to any of this talk about you not being your mind—as it clearly wants to remain in charge. In fact, it will never stop preaching to you from the pulpit of the two reasons. Yet even as it does, knowing that the power is in your hands, you must totally disregard pretty much everything your mind has to say!

Knowing this, think back to any time you did something you wish you hadn't—and no matter what or how long it may take—immediately commit to making things right as opposed to allowing that mistake (or any other mistakes you made because you were listening to your mind), to continue to exist as proof that you're not good enough.

Consciousness is never about playing it safe or learning how to avoid making mistakes; it's about embracing the fact that even when you do fall into reaction, it's simply proof that you're human versus the false conclusion that there's something wrong with you or you don't have what it takes. Again, you were born with what it takes!

In the end, mastery is a function of knowing that it's fully within your power to override your instincts; *first* by refusing to listen to your mind, *then* by aligning with both your inner magician and your inner warrior in favor of making your dreams come true.

In support of this intention, I invite you to allow the following teachings to inspire you to shine all the light in your heart on what's possible once you do.

Chapter 3 Teachings

3.1

Your job is to make magic happen. Your mind's job is to be on the lookout for trouble. Mastery, therefore, is a function of allowing your mind to do its job while you're doing yours. The secret to creating the life of your dreams is to bring your inner magician along for the ride and to stop focusing on the potholes!

At the end of the day, joyfulness is for those who get lost in what they're creating and in their service to others—not in their fears.

"Our mind is enriched by what we receive, our heart by what we give."
—Victor Hugo

Given that it's your mind's job is to steer you clear of challenges—yet success is a result of overcoming them instead—it will serve you to ignore just about everything your mind has to say. Fortunately, although you can't turn your mind off, you can override it. Mastery is for those who do.

3.2

Only by overriding your desire to prove how great you are—otherwise known as trying too hard—will you be empowered to show up as the fully capable human being you were born to be.

Unless and until you embrace the truth of your inherent magnificence, you'll forever feel the need to prove yourself to everyone, rather than leave them inspired by who you truly are.

Mastery is for those who override their ego's need to try to *appear* competent with an intention to simply *be* competent instead.

Remember, it's your ego that others tend to find annoying—not you.

"A superior man is modest in his speech but exceeds in his actions."
—Confucius

Intentionality is a function of overriding your mind's desire for you to appear to be who you wish you were with simply showing up as who you already are. Once you surrender to the truth of your inherent magnificence, you'll realize that you—being you—is all you ever need to be.

3.3

Although it's normal for our survival instinct to steer us clear of situations we perceive as threats, anything we are actively avoiding tends to live as a troll beneath the bridge to our dreams. Unfortunately, no matter how scary that sucker may be, until you make friends with your troll, you'll find it all but impossible for you to cross that bridge.

Success, therefore, is for those who embrace whatever they're avoiding and face their fears head-on, rather than waiting for them to subside. Once you honor your courage more than the troll, you'll be amazed at how quickly your dreams come true.

"Change is never painful, only your resistance to change is painful."
—Zen proverb

What part of you are you making wrong? What gifts aren't you using? Where do you justify playing small? Remember, if you catch yourself doing any of these things, it's simply proof that you are human; it's not an indication that you don't have what it takes. Embrace your humanity, know that it's fully within you to step beyond it, and then march your butt across that bridge.

3.4

Your ego is an imposter pretending to be you. Accordingly, only by paying no attention at all to the imposter will you be able to replace your mind's inclination to dominate and control others with a loving intention to serve and empower them instead.

No matter what your little voice is whispering in your ear, only by choosing *service* over *ego* will you not only be empowered to inspire others to shine their own light a little brighter, who you truly are will shine even brighter as well.

"To be a person you're not is to waste the amazing person you are."
—Loren Lahav

Whether you allow your voice to serve as a loudspeaker for your ego or as a messenger of your heart is always up to you. Miracles are for those who let love and authenticity do their talking.

3.5

Plain and simple, the biological function of the human mind is survival, which means its primary purpose is to ensure that you avoid any and all situations where your ego might take a hit. Even so, although you clearly have a mind, you are not your mind, so it's always your call as to whether you surrender to your instincts or choose to live on purpose.

As you can imagine, your mind isn't at all happy with you discovering this truth, as it was hoping you would make it all the way to checkout without learning of your ability to override what it wants you to do. In other words, know that you have a choice.

Consciousness is for those who know they have a choice. Mastery is for those who make the right choice.

"He who knows others is wise. He who knows himself is enlightened."
—Lao Tzu

There's no joy in taking what you do for granted or in simply getting by. Joyfulness is for those who honor their passion more than their instincts and bring it with them wherever they go.

3.6

Energetically, we are all inextricably connected at the most fundamental level of consciousness. And yet, our ability to experience ourselves as such depends upon whether we're driven by love or fear.

Unfortunately, since our instincts prompt us to feel fear, we're inclined to go where our mind want us to go, allowing it to stand guard at the door to our heart. Sadly, even though our door guard is unarmed, he's scary as hell and talks a good game, so instead of challenging him, most of us simply surrender and allow him to run the show.

Still, even as we're compelled to give in, it's forever within us to honor our intention rather than our door guard, so it's always up to us to shine our light as brightly as we can on each other.

The only way to influence anyone who is still being held captive by their survival mind is to plant a seed of love—even as their door guard is doing all it can to turn us away.

Remember, what you're dealing with is fear, not evil.

> 'Rule your mind or it will rule you."
> —Buddha

Whether your journey through life is an ego trip or a spirit quest is totally up to you. Mastery is for those who refuse to bring anything less than their full intention along for the ride.

3.7

Given that we are basically animals (mammals), with the ability to talk and worry, most of us are living lives where these two specific skill sets are forever getting us into trouble.

Hence, the key to achieving all the success and happiness you deserve is to focus on doing whatever you are doing as excellently as you can— while paying no attention to anything your survival mind is whispering in your ear.

Success is for those who appreciate their minds for what they are—but are wise enough to never allow them to run the show.

> "It is the mark of an educated mind to be able to
> entertain a thought without accepting it."
> —Aristotle

Wisdom is for those who refuse to concern themselves with every little thing that could go wrong. Worrying causes your imagination to create things you don't want. If you imagine things going right, you'll attract that instead.

3.8

Contrary to what the culture has hypnotized us into believing, confidence and certainty are actually states of mind, which all of us have the ability to access and bring forth simply because we say so (as opposed to being fleeting emotions, which we may or may not have access to, depending upon how we're feeling).

In other words, if ever you are feeling any uncertainty at all, by simply taking ownership of your humanity (accepting that you have fallen prey to your reactionary mind and then refusing to stay there), you'll be inspired to unleash all your intention and power at will.

"He who conquers others is strong. He who conquers himself is mighty."
—Zen proverb

Once you give up the notion that your confidence is tied to the ebb and flow of forces beyond your own creation, you'll be free to access your inherent certainty simply because you can.

It's our conditioning and beliefs that keep us small and not what we've identified as lacking.

Mastery, therefore, is for those who replace searching for whatever they feel is missing with simply unleashing it instead.

3.9

As human beings, all of us were born inherently worthy. And yet, due to our natural tendency to question ourselves, we're inclined to wonder just how worthy we truly are. In fact, this is why most of us so often feel like we're pretending to be something we're not, which is why we tend to worry in the first place.

Fortunately, in spite of this natural inclination to worry, mastery is for those who honor their inherent worthiness more than their worry-ness and appreciate that the truth will show up in spades—once they are intentionally bringing it to the party—rather than waiting for it to show up. Once you're willing to see things as they really are, you'll have absolutely no reason to doubt yourself at all.

"You must lose the battle of being right to win the war of being happy."
—Auriela McCarthy

The ability to know yourself as fully worthy isn't something you attain from outside yourself, and it is not going to magically show up once you accumulate enough proof.
You were born worthy. Begin there.

3.10

Although we've all been taught to embrace our feelings, if you're feeling anything other than fully aligned with what you know in your heart will serve you, your feelings are the last place you should be looking for evidence of what you're capable of achieving.
In spite of how uncertain we may be at times, success is for those who know that no matter how unsure we feel when taking on something new, taking action first will make us feel more certain.

"Our greatest enemies, the ones we must fight most often, are within."
—Thomas Paine

Mastery is for those who replace waking up in reaction to how they're feeling with waking up already knowing how they're going to show up.

3.11

Whether or not you choose to override your fight-or-flight programming and assume full responsibility for your life is totally up to you.
Clearly, although there's certainly nothing wrong with allowing your subconscious mind to lead you around by the nose, wisdom is for those who are clear about what they want and why they want it and who refuse to settle for anything less.
At the end of the day, if you've been waiting for what you want to show up on its own, all you'll ever achieve is the realization that it didn't show up while you were sitting around waiting.

"Wherever you go, go with all your heart."
—Confucius

Life is a treasure hunt, yet if you simply allow things to unfold as they may, you have no right to expect anything more of tomorrow than to wake up another day older.

3.12

No matter how optimistic you're trying to be, since the default setting of being human is *doubtful,* the subconscious mind is always on the lookout for reasons why we should be more careful. For this reason, the next time you catch yourself reacting to your fear of not being enough, it will serve you to remain intentional and know that this is simply your mind doing its job. Even though living in reaction to this fear is normal, it's certainly not a recipe for turning any optimism you do have into success.
Therefore, it will serve you even more to refuse to listen to your mind and to think and act in favor of your vision and your purpose.
How to Override Your Mind

    A. create a meaningful purpose
    B. pursue equally meaningful goals and outcomes
    C. show up in alignment with your intention rather than your fear

Once you refuse to let anything stop you from living on purpose, you'll discover that creating the life of your dreams is as easy as A-B-C.

"Fear is a reaction. Courage is a decision."
—Sir Winston Churchill

Most of us create excuses for our failures even before we fail. Success is for those who prepare a victory speech instead.

3.13

So many of us have trouble bringing all we've got to everything we do because the ego considers it a win whenever we're able to convince the right people that we're bringing our full intention to the party—even though we're actually doing just enough to get by.

In fact, we tend to expend more energy trying to appear as though we're playing full-out than we would if we simply did so.

At the end of the day, the greatest success is for those who say no to their egos—while refusing to bring anything less than their absolute best to everything they do—and continue to play full-out until everything they want shows up.

> "Those who cannot change their minds cannot change anything."
> —George Bernard Shaw

Although all of us are inclined to doubt ourselves at times, success is for those who refuse to honor their minds, which are doing the doubting, more than their ability to override them.

3.14

Although it would appear that we are in charge of our own psychology, our survival mind is actually running the show and devoting all of its time to steering us clear of danger.

Even when your mind perceives a threat and prompts you to avoid it, it's still fully within your power to remain focused on what you intend to accomplish, even as your little voice (the fear of looking foolish) is imploring you to rethink your plans.

Mastery, therefore, is for those who actually accept that the mind is going to vote no more often than not—yet who have no intention at all of ever listening to it.

> "You are responsible for the energy you bring to this world.
> Fear dims your Light and Love raises you to exude the

vibration of the Heavens. Choose to create heaven on this
earth and pioneer the greatest ascension of humanity."
—Nancy Penttila Lemire

Although all of us were born with fear, we were also born with the ability to step beyond it. Success, therefore, is for those who honor their intention more than what they're afraid of and refuse to grant their mind the right to vote.

3.15

The ego-mind stands guard at the door to your soul, preventing access to your true self.
Listening to your ego will impede your ability to love as deeply as you can and your ability to express your "you-ness" as fully as possible into the universe. Therefore, if your intention is to live as authentically and joyfully as possible, you must immediately fire your door guard.
All the love you can ever imagine is available to you once who do.

"Stop acting so small. You are the universe in ecstatic motion."
—Rumi

Mastery is never about acquiring something you perceive to be missing from beyond yourself; it's about stepping beyond whatever's preventing you from showing up as who you already are.

3.16

The universe adores you and is totally aligned with your grandest, most heartfelt intentions. As for being enamored with your ego, not so much. Which path you take is always up to you, but only by intentionally overriding your ego and choosing to live in alignment with your heart will the universe begin to shine a light on your path.

On the other hand, should you continue to strive for dominance at the expense of others—even as your ego continues to blow smoke up your butt—it won't be long before you realize you're going it alone.

> "If you decide to trust your mind, you will surely come to regret it. When you decide to trust your heart, you'll never look back."
> —Erica Nitti Becker

Freedom is for those who let go of everything they feel they no longer need. Mastery is for those who let go of their attachment to everything they feel they can't live without. Once you accept that all you truly need is already within you, that's all you really need to know.

Chapter 3 Key Concept

What you tell yourself you are, you will become. What you tell yourself you are not, you'll never become. Who do you want to be today? What if it really is this easy?

> "When you change, the world around you changes. You have that much power."
> —Niurka

Section I Exercises
Turning Awareness into Action

Living in alignment with "the truth." Learning to say no to your "little voice." How to step into your power instead of allowing your survival mind to run the show.

1. What are you withholding from others? Actions? Emotions? Be specific with examples: "I am withholding love from my partner," "I withhold my full connection to friends," "I am withholding the pursuit of my passion," etc.
2. What are the reasons you withhold in these areas of your life?
3. What are your biggest life regrets? How could these be life lessons instead? What did they teach you? Did they change your path for the better? How could they?
4. Name specific ways that you take responsibility for feeling happy and fulfilled each day. If you don't, how will you do so from now on?
5. Who are you? Who are you not? Who do you intend to show up as from now on?
6. How committed are you to catching yourself in reaction and shifting back into intention? To what degree are you committed to living this way? How will this change your life?

    Who is in charge of you?

SECTION II

Expansion and Growth

Focusing on what you want, where you are going, and what's possible. By the end of this section, you will have discovered the key to creating your Vision and Purpose!

I.   Limiting Beliefs; Overcoming the Fear of not being good enough
II.   Letting go of the Past; Giving yourself the gift of Freedom!
III. Vision and Passion! Showing up as the Superstar you were born to be!

Section II Exercises: Turning Freedom into Action
Overriding your limiting beliefs. Stepping beyond whatever is keeping those beliefs in place. Declaring your Vision and Purpose in support of making your dreams come true, including how to forgive yourself and others.

CHAPTER 4

Limiting Beliefs

Overcoming the Fear of Not Being Good Enough

What is your single most disempowering limiting belief? How does it hold you back?

If you could replace it with a more empowering belief, what would that be?

Who would you need to become in order to believe that instead?

> "There is nothing good or bad but thinking makes it so."
> —William Shakespeare

Mastery has nothing to do with finding what's missing or fixing what's broken. It's about letting go of whatever's stopping you from showing up as the superstar you were born to be.

When was the last time you thought about doing anything at all beyond what you felt comfortable doing without second-guessing yourself in some way? In other words, when did you last consider taking on anything new, buying something of significant value, or doing anything you normally wouldn't do without having any second thoughts or rethinking your plans before doing anything worth doing? In fact, because it's totally normal not to, when was the last time you spent any quality time at all outside your comfort zone?

Remember, since the primary purpose of the mind is to steer you clear of danger, the only reason your mind even created a comfort zone in the first place was to allow you to notice when you're no longer in it.

Therefore, whenever it senses that you're about to do anything where your ego might take a hit, it will not only have you rethink whatever you're about to do, it will question what the hell you're even doing outside your comfort zone in the first place; preferring instead that you pay a lot more attention to what *it* wants you to believe than to anything that might get you into trouble.

However, even though you're now an expert on how your mind works—which includes knowing that although you can't turn it off you can override it—there are still a couple of things it will serve you to know in support of you ultimately stepping beyond your beliefs:

1. Limiting beliefs are not real, which is why they're called beliefs and not *truths*.
2. You have every ability to totally disregard them on the way to creating the life of your dreams.

To begin to leave those limiting beliefs behind, think back to a specific goal you wanted to achieve in the past, but then decided to call it quits—either because you changed your mind before you took any action at all, or you did give it a shot, but then gave up as after listening to your little voice. And although *giving up* seemed like a good idea at the time, quitting left you feeling like you're not good enough—both because you clearly felt it was true at the time, and because you're still holding onto it, not only as proof, but as part of your collection.

No matter what your mind is holding onto from the past, whenever you are motivated to take action to achieve something you desire, there are actually only two options available to you in any given moment:

A. You go for it.
B. You don't.

And when you don't, it's pretty much tied to one reason and one reason only: your limiting beliefs.

In other words, when you decide to put off the pursuit of a specific outcome, it has nothing at all to do with falling prey to what we've been conditioned to call procrastination—or because you've somehow lost your motivation—it's that you're simply being influenced by memories of things that have stopped you before (which are really nothing other than limiting beliefs). After all, if there's anything on your to do-list you truly want to do, would you ever not do it on purpose? Of course not. So, if you ever stop doing what you otherwise want to do, it's because you are both living in reaction to your limiting beliefs *and* allowing your reactive mind to run the show.

Again, it's never what you feel you're afraid of that's stopping you, it's that you're living in reaction to whatever your mind is whispering in your ear. Therefore, the first step to overcoming your limiting beliefs is to own the fact that to be human includes the inclination to allow the memory of any situation where you fell short in the past to live within your mind as a limiting belief. This is not only normal; it's a by-product of your humanity. Therefore, your limiting beliefs are never proof that there's anything wrong with you; they're simply proof that you *think* there is.

What's more, since your limiting beliefs are really nothing more than memories, and since your memories are really nothing more than your opinions about how things *were*, at the end of the day, your memories are really nothing more than thoughts. So, there's no reason not to appreciate them as background noise rather than holding onto them as proof that you're not good enough. This is also why you have every ability to simply *have* memories instead of allowing your memories to have you—and especially why it will serve you to simply let them be.

Yes. Let them be. Embrace your humanity, but never forget that since anything you resist persists, it's our very trying to do away with our fears and limiting beliefs that actually inspires them to dig in their heels. But once you do stop resisting, you'll find that the real problem is never what you've identified as a limiting belief; it's that you're allowing it to stop you by believing it's true. That's the problem.

In fact, even if it's true that there are things you don't know, or even if you're lacking a specific skill or ability, you simply need to learn it and run with it. No matter how much any of us know or don't know, even when we do make a mistake, it's never proof that we're not good enough; it's simply proof that we're human. And because we are human, we have no control over our minds turning our setbacks into limiting beliefs. We perceive these beliefs as limiting, but the only reason the mind creates them in the first place is to keep us safe. Afterall, if it's able to convince us that we're not good enough, then it has clearly done its job.

Even so, it's never our limiting beliefs that stop us; it's the underlying belief that we should actually quit when they tell us to quit that stops us. A belief that exists solely as a result of you buying into the most fundamental of all limiting beliefs—that something that isn't even happening in the moment—can somehow affect how you are showing up right now. And although this dynamic tends to rob us of our intention, this is nothing but an annoying little scam your mind is forever running in the background, as it would prefer that you simply tiptoe timidly through the rest of your life. Fortunately, since you are not your mind, you have literally been blessed with the ability to take much bigger steps!

So, are you ready to start taking bigger steps? Your limiting beliefs are simply beliefs, not truths, so the only thing that's ever really stopping you is your belief that they're true. Since our limiting beliefs are simply doors to the things we've yet to achieve and the dreams we've yet to dream, most of us never attempt to open these doors because, when we're living in reaction, they all appear to be locked. In actuality, they are only closed.

Since we spend so much time perceiving our limiting beliefs as locked doors, even when we do take action in pursuit of something we want, the moment our underlying belief that we're not good enough kicks in, we're inclined to perceive that we don't have what it takes to find the keys. When we're living in reaction to this belief, we also tend to believe that it would take a ridiculous amount of time to earn or otherwise obtain the key to the door we want—and that we'd first have to figure out which door to go for.

In reaction to this line of thinking, a feeling of being overwhelmed sets in, and we tend to think that with so many doors to choose from, perhaps it might be easier to simply forget all this mastery stuff in the hope that someday, the right door will finally reveal itself—along with the key.

Is this starting to sound familiar? After all, this wouldn't be the first time you felt this way or wondered why you feel like giving up as often as you do. Yet you mustn't forget that these are not *your* thoughts. It's your mind tapping you on the shoulder, pointing out that all your doors are locked, reminding you that you're not good enough, and imploring you to play it safe by simply hanging out in the hallway. Whew!

Breaking news! Your mind *is* your door guard. And since his primary job is survival, he's pretty much been on high alert ever since you started reading this book, feeding you as many limiting beliefs as he needs to in order to keep you mired in self-doubt—all for the purpose of keeping you small and safe. Therefore, unless you convince him that you are in charge, he will interpret everything you're learning about mastery as a threat to your survival, warn you that you shouldn't believe everything you read, and try to convince you to stop reading and do something else. After all, your imminent freedom is making your door guard very nervous right now.

Remember, it's his job to steer you away from anything he perceives as a threat. Yet since he's essentially a con artist who simply talks a good game, I promise you that it's fully within your power to call your door guard's bluff and walk right past him. After all, it's your door.

More breaking news- None of the doors to your future are locked. Therefore, it's never about making your limiting beliefs disappear; it's about ignoring them as the lies they are until your door guard finally gets a clue and realizes that it's time for him to start listening to you.

And since the purpose of this chapter has been to redirect your focus from anything that's been stopping you to what lies before you, I invite you to allow the following teachings to finally shine a light on what's possible once you're willing to "call fraud" on both your mind and your limiting beliefs.

Chapter 4 Teachings

4.1

If there are things in your life that consistently show up as lacking, it's more than likely because you've come to expect them to be lacking. In fact, all that's really lacking is your beliefs and expectations.

Unless and until you raise your expectations, the universe will continue to send all that it is holding in escrow for you to someone with higher expectations. Fortunately, once you step beyond your limiting beliefs, not only will the universe welcome you home, everything you deserve will start flowing in your direction.

We have been conditioned to believe in things only when we perceive them to be true, but in reality, it's other way around.

> "You'll see it when you believe it."
> —Wayne Dyer

The first step toward believing that you can is to acknowledge that you've been brainwashed into believing that you can't. When you upgrade your beliefs, you upgrade your life. Fortunately, what you believe is totally up to you. Believe wisely.

4.2

Thanks to our survival instinct, we tend to worry about every little thing. Only by refocusing all of your intentional energy on making your dreams come true will you be inspired to ignore your little voice when it's telling you that you're not good enough, which would otherwise continue to rob you of your confidence and certainty.

All of us have doubts, yet until you override yours with intention and faith, they will continue to live within your mind as disappointments that are waiting to happen.

Remember, success isn't reserved for those without any doubts; it's for those who refuse to let any doubts they do have stand in their way.

> "Within you right now is the power to do things you never
> even dreamed possible. This power becomes available to
> you just as soon as you can change your beliefs."
> —Maxwell Maltz

In every moment, we are either inspired by what we believe to be possible or dismayed by our belief in what isn't. Fortunately, you are fully in charge of what you believe—so I invite you to believe in you.

4.3

One man watches a sunset and is in awe. Another simply sees the sun going down. Although all of us are literally wired to resist looking on the bright side of things, within each of us exists the ability to step beyond our wiring and appreciate the inherent wonder in every little thing, including ourselves. Once you intentionally override your default inclination to focus on what you perceive to be lacking—by focusing instead on everything that isn't lacking—all the joy in the universe will be yours.

> "We are what we think. All that we are arises with our
> thoughts. With our thoughts we make our world."
> —Buddha

How much sunshine did you share with others today? Or were you focusing on the clouds instead? No matter what you perceive to be missing, the degree to which you're able to appreciate and celebrate everything else is forever up to you. Knowing this is consciousness. Living it is bliss.

4.4

Transformation is a process of accessing what's already present within you and then bringing that forth, whether you believe it's fully within you or not. In fact, not only will it serve you to give up wondering if you have what it takes, it will serve you even more to give up looking for proof that you don't.

No matter what you believe, you were *born* with what it takes, so unleashing your full potential is a function of refusing to be held hostage by the belief that anything you feel you're lacking is somehow holding you back.

Mastery is for those who have called off the search for what they believe is missing and accepted that the only thing that's truly missing is their willingness to accept that nothing's missing.

> "To find yourself, think for yourself."
> —Socrates

Joyfulness is for those who replace waking up worried about what the day is going to bring with waking up already knowing what they are going to bring to the day.

4.5

The culture has hypnotized us into believing that passion is scarce, and that happiness is something that must be pursued. After all, the Declaration of Independence grants all Americans the right to pursue happiness, yet how many times have we been told that we can't have our cake and eat it too? No matter what we've been told, only by choosing to give up the belief that your power is tied to the ebb and flow of forces beyond yourself will you be inspired to unleash all your inherent joy and passion at will.

Although it will serve you to surround yourself with like-minded souls and otherwise set yourself up to win, it's our cultural conditioning that robs us of our aliveness—not our circumstances.

"Reexamine all that you've been told. Dismiss what insults your soul."
—Walt Whitman

Joyfulness is for those who bring passion along for the ride rather than hoping it shows up once they get to where they're going.

4.6

Motivation is what shows up when you marry a burning desire with a powerful intention and then refuse to invite fear and doubt to the wedding. If ever you're feeling less than turned on by what you're currently doing, you have either lost sight of your purpose or are focusing instead on the reasons why you're not achieving it (either of which will rob you of your passion). Once you embrace who you truly are and then shine more light on the reasons why you want what you want than you do on what you perceive to be missing, you will be inspired to take massive action in pursuit of your dreams, and the universe will be inspired to shine a light on your path.

"A powerful intention trumps motivation any day.
Instead of wishing you felt motivated, it will serve you
to create a purposeful intent and live from that!"
—Erica Nitti Becker

Unless you step boldly beyond the things that are holding you back, you'll likely settle for less than you deserve—while achieving even less than you expect. Fortunately, although it's normal for life's challenges to turn you off, it's fully within you to turn yourself back on.

4.7

Although all of us tend to feel stuck at times, it's never our circumstances that are holding us back; it's what we're telling ourselves about our circumstances. No matter what's going on around you, motivation is a function of believing in who you are and what's possible rather than in your opinions about what isn't.

Wisdom is for those who are as quick to take ownership of their limiting opinions as they are to apologize to anyone who may have been caught in the crossfire, including themselves.

"Do not seek the truth, only cease to cherish your opinions."
—Zen proverb

"Our beliefs our what drive our lives. Get the Truth on what
you believe and the whole game changes. You win!"
—Claudette Anderson

No matter what we perceive to be standing in our way, it's not that we can't see what we're not seeing; it's that we can't see that we aren't seeing what we're not seeing.

4.8

Success is for those who have no interest at all in waiting for someday. Even so, only by calling off the search for whatever you feel is missing will you discover that everything you need is already within you. Energetically, it's always a function of what you're focusing on and how you're showing up that ultimately determines how likely you are to succeed.

Fortunately, whether you allow your future to be shaped by the things you're committed to or by the things you're afraid of is always up to you. With our thoughts, we shape our worlds. Shape wisely.

> "Very little is needed to make a happy life; it is all
> within yourself, in your way of thinking."
> —Marcus Aurelius

Passion is your birthright, but if you pay more attention to what's robbing you of it than you do to what turns you on, you'll never see the forest of what's possible through the trees of your despair.

4.9

> "Out beyond ideas of wrong and right, there
> is a field. I will meet you there."
> —Rumi

If ever you find yourself stuck in a deteriorating situation, although your first inclination may be to throw someone under the bus, what will actually save the day is to focus on a solution rather than trying to figure out who's to blame. Success is for those who devote more time to resolving challenges than they do to lamenting them, and who take solace in knowing that there's a lesson in every setback and a blessing in every lesson.

Mastery is for those who are on the lookout for lessons rather than scapegoats.

"A powerful attitude allows you to take ownership of
your situation. You acknowledge and accept your role
and now have the ability to change its course."
—Evy Poumpouras

We are fully in charge of how we show up in every moment. Although challenges are a part of life, suffering is optional. Since you would never suffer on purpose, suffering can only show up when you're not living on purpose. Freedom is for those who live on purpose.

4.10

Leaders strive for excellence and not approval. Mastery, therefore, is for those who are looking to make a difference rather than for evidence of their worthiness. In fact, since there's no energetic connection at all between reality and what we are feeling, if you're okay with waiting until you feel like it before taking action, you'll likely be waiting a long damn time.
At the end of the day, happiness is a function of accepting that everything you've been waiting for is actually waiting for you to give up the wait.
All the joy imaginable is for those who are willing to replace waiting with playing full-out.

"The world rewards those who take responsibility for their own success."
—Curt Gerrish

Certainty isn't a feeling you attain from beyond yourself, nor is it going to magically appear once you accumulate enough proof. In actuality, certainty is already within you; waiting for you to rid yourself of all the reasons why you're not feeling it. Obliterate your reasons. Be certain.

4.11

Contrary to popular belief, confidence and certainty are really nothing other than intentional states of being, which we have every ability to access and bring to the party simply because we can.

In other words, the ability to show up *on purpose* is essentially no more complicated than 1) knowing that it's fully within you to shift your state at will, 2) being willing to apologize for any mess you made while you were in reaction, and 3) owning your ability to step into your power, and then proactively doing so. No matter how much uncertainty you feel at times, once you take full ownership of your psychology, showing up in an intentional state is as easy as 1-2-3.

> "Life isn't about finding yourself. Life is about creating yourself."
> —George Bernard Shaw

Raising your standards is a good thing, but unless you also raise your expectations, you may earn lots of praise—but nothing you can actually take to the bank.

4.12

At the most fundamental level of consciousness, we are not only inherently equal; we were born inherently worthy as well (even though we also share an inherent fear that we're not).

Once you embrace these truths, you'll be inspired to override your fear of not being good enough and your equally inherent (and equally annoying) need to prove yourself to everyone.

Even though it's totally normal to feel uncertain at times, it's still very much within you to step beyond your fears and shine your light as brightly as you possibly can.

At the end of the day, although all of us popped out of the womb inherently worthy, happiness will continue to elude you if you continue to spend your time looking for proof that you're not.

> "Oh God, help me believe the truth about myself,
> no matter how beautiful it is. Amen."
> —Macrina Wiederkehr

The secret to life is to replace hoping to become who you wish you were with simply being who you already are. Once you embrace and fully unleash your inherent magnificence, falling in love with yourself is inevitable.

4.13

As a result of growing up in a results-driven culture, not only are we inclined to be *do-ers* rather than *be-ers,* most of the things we do tend to impede our ability to both stop and smell the roses and fully appreciate how wonderful life really is. Once you acknowledge your conditioning and override it with an intention to be fully present to *everything* you do—while also doing it as excellently as you can—you'll realize that you're able to smell the roses as you go!

No matter what your conditioning is whispering in your ear, consciousness is for those who honor their ability to *do* and *be* at the very same time.

> "Every time you have to ask for permission to live the life of your dreams, you lose energy from your most trusted power source: you!"
> —Erica Nitti Becker

Once you accept that you are not your feelings or your beliefs, they will no longer have any power over you. This being said, when would now be a good time to do so?

4.14

The chances of creating the life of your dreams without really expecting it to happen are about the same as striking oil while digging a hole in your backyard. Success is for those with the wisdom to replace hope with *action* and doubt with *faith,* and then truly expect everything they're doing to pay off.

Frankly, there is no such thing as "reasonable" doubt because our limiting beliefs and limiting expectations—disguised as doubt—tend to thwart our intention at every turn.

No matter how much *hope* you bring to the party, unless you're also expecting your dreams to come true, you'll likely be dreaming forever.

"If you want a certain thing, first be a certain person. Then obtaining that certain thing will no longer be of concern."
—Zen proverb

If you truly intend to succeed, I invite you to give up all hope. Give it up—and replace it with faith. Hope inspires waiting. Faith inspires action. If you truly want the universe to align with your intention, you must give it something to align with. Stop hoping. Start expecting.

4.15

No one will ever believe in you more than you believe in yourself. And yet, only by giving up worrying about what others may be thinking will you be inspired to have faith in all that you do. Inspiration is for those who spend more time looking to make a difference than they do hoping to make a good impression.

At the end of the day, if you truly intend to inspire others to feel more confident in your abilities, it's never about what you're doing; it's about how you're showing up. Fortunately, by simply accessing your inherent certainty, you'll show up just fine.

"If you want to fly, give up everything that's weighing you down."
—Buddha

Confidence is a function of bringing certainty along for the ride rather than hoping it shows up once you get to where you're going.

4.16

As a result of what we have been hypnotized into believing while growing up, most of us tend to accept that we should avoid "counting our chickens before they hatch" or "putting all our eggs in one basket." And then, once we finally do decide what to do, it would be crazy to even think of doing anything until all our ducks are in a row.

Whether or not you're conscious of these influences, only by being willing to accept that walking around hypnotized is probably not the best way to continue living your life will you be free to pursue new possibilities you would have previously considered crazy.

So… are you okay with remaining married to your conditioning—or are you willing to give crazy a try?

When it comes to making things happen, we are either waiting for them to happen or blazing a trail of our own. I invite you to start blazing.

> "Unless you try or do something beyond what you
> have already mastered, you will never grow."
> —Ralph Waldo Emerson

Whether you allow your beliefs to limit your challenges or step beyond them and challenge your limits is forever up to you. Success is for those who live from their hearts and not their conditioning.

4.17

All of us have been conditioned to believe that it's better to be safe than sorry, yet it's *much better* to be courageous—for which you'll never be sorry. In fact, while succumbing to one's fears has never been acknowledged by anyone who has ever achieved anything as the secret to their success, determination truly is the breakfast of champions!

No matter what you're looking to accomplish, once you allow intention to pull you out of bed, and then start your day with a bowl of courage, all you've ever wanted will be yours.

> "He who conquers others is strong. He who conquers himself is mighty."
> —Zen proverb

In the wake of any setback, mastery is for those who are quicker to forgive and forget than they are to lament what went wrong. Beating yourself up is no substitute for simply letting things go.

Chapter 4 Key Concept

Believing in yourself is the highest level of motivation and inspiration. Never stop doing so!

"When you realize there is nothing lacking,
the whole world belongs to you."
—Lao Tzu

CHAPTER 5

Letting Go of the Past

Giving yourself the gift of Freedom

To what degree are you allowing your past to run your life right now?

If you had a magic wand, what are the top three memories you'd like to replace with new empowering beliefs? What would those new beliefs be—and how would you feel once you did?

> "Let go of the past, go for the future. Go confidently in the direction of your dreams. Live the life you imagined."
> —Henry David Thoreau

Mastery is for those who are willing to question what they think, as well as where it is they are thinking it from. Energetically, once you let go of your past, your past will let go of you.

So, what's your story? Even if you're not sure—or are simply unable to define it in words—I assure you that you have one. Of course, you may not be thinking of it in terms of a story. Perhaps you've simply been calling it life, since for many of us, it's simply a willingness to dance with whatever shows up while avoiding all the drama.

In the wake of surviving anything that was even the slightest bit traumatic, I promise you that your mind has been quick to add that event to the unique and significant story it's been writing on your behalf, perhaps casting you as the star, but not as the hero you should be. And since there's a lot more in it for your mind to have written a drama than a documentary, I assure you that with regard to everything it has written so far, it has been featuring all of your traumatic memories as the main plot of your story.

What's more it's been doing so with no recognition at all of you as the hero you've been in overcoming them—even though it's very clear that you truly are a hero. In other words, it's been writing more of a tearjerker than any testament at all to your courage.

However, once you're willing to take ownership of everything you now know and accept that it's totally in your power to fire your door guard and replace him with you as the author of your life, you'll know that there's absolutely nothing at all stopping you from going anywhere in life you decide to go.

To focus more clearly on where you're going, you must finally own up to any drama you've been leaving in your wake, remaining fully aware of the fact that it all went down while your mind was running the show. And since it was, wouldn't its story have had a victim with his or her share of conflicts and challenges? Well, your story surely did, but now that you are in charge, there's no reason to accept any input from either your mind, your limiting beliefs, or your past. In fact, there is nothing at all left to stop you from creating the life you deserve!

Although we all have memories of surviving trauma, the story we've been telling ourselves about it (in other words, the "sob story" your mind has likely been calling your story), is simply your ego allowing you to feel sorry for yourself while keeping you immersed in all the drama. So, unless this is where you want to stay, now would be the perfect time to start writing a story of your own.

Again, if you allow yourself to see what's really going on, you'll realize that there's only one thing stopping you from letting go of any of your painful memories, and that's the story you've been unconsciously telling yourself about them.

The only reason any of us continue to hold onto anything painful about the past is because we survived it. In fact, any event that you survived but are having trouble erasing from your memory is really nothing more than that—a memory, which means that in and of itself, it's simply an enigma wrapped in a belief, signifying nothing other than the fact that your memory is working just fine.

Now that you know you've been holding onto this memory as proof that you're not good enough—and even storing it as part of a collection of lots of other similar memories—here's a question for you: could it be that the reason you've been having trouble letting go of feeling bad about any specific memory isn't so much about that memory but the fact that feeling bad is actually tied to a larger collection of proof from the past that you're not good enough?

Well, let me help you out here: yes! That is clearly why you tend to feel bad when anything reminds you of your unpleasant memories. It has very little to do with any specific memory, but the fact that you are continuously being reminded of an entire lifetime full of proof that you're not good enough! However, since you now know it's nothing but a limiting belief that you aren't good enough, this entire collection of what your mind has been calling proof is simply proof of one thing and one thing only: you are human.

In fact, if we could look inside your head, we wouldn't find any limiting beliefs swimming around in there. We wouldn't find this so-called collection of proof, which is because the only thing your mind has ever been holding onto is this giant collection of thoughts that don't serve you—and for no other reason than that's its job!

Letting go is a function of accepting the fact that what's really holding you back is nothing more than your reaction to a bunch of totally random thoughts, tied solely to your survival instinct, which have absolutely nothing to do with your inherent worthiness. Nothing!

Clearly, the past no longer exists, so the *first* step in letting it go is to simply embrace the fact that it isn't even here. Seriously. It's not. That means whenever you feel stuck in the past, all that's really going on is that you are showing up *in reaction* to a story that your mind is holding onto about something that's no longer happening rather than acknowledging the hero you are for having survived it.

Frankly, if you're willing to see what's so, you'll notice that even when you do win, you rarely celebrate the fact that you succeeded in the face of a perceived threat because your mind was too busy focusing on the threat rather than on what you did to survive it, which you obviously did since you're still here!

Once you're willing to own how heroic you are for having overcome all that you have, the *second* step to breaking free of the past is to replace the story your mind made up about you being a victim with the truth of how you overcame it. Acknowledge that your victim story was the booby prize and that your new story—the grand prize, and the only one that truly matters—is the one where you're the Hero. Because it's true!

Now that you know you own the ability to let go of every story that isn't serving you, it's fully within your power to do so and replace each one with a victory speech once you do. After all, no matter what you've had to endure, you still survived it all. Therefore, I invite you to start writing a new story about everything you intend to accomplish, including working on that victory speech.

Yes, a victory speech. For even though embracing your power has nothing to do with ego, the *third* step in breaking free is knowing that by willfully letting go of your old story, you are also showing up as your own hero in letting go of your past. And once you let go of your past, *it* will let go of you.

Remember, the only reason your mind created a story in the first place was in reaction to a situation where it perceived you as a victim. And although the star of that story is whomever it was who hurt you, your mind has no use at all for you forgiving them. That would cost you a piece of proof from your collection—the one that *your mind* is using to keep you from doing anything dumb—but is really keeping you mired in self-doubt.

The only way to override feeling like a victim is to accept that all of us are essentially victims of other victims. You are never alone in feeling this way, as it's totally normal to do so. Of course, this doesn't justify any of the trauma you have had to deal with, but it does explain it.

As you stand in the light of this understanding rather than continuing to live in the shadow of any unresolved resentments, I invite you to create a list of everyone with whom you feel it will serve you to make amends. Then, in support of leaving your past behind, keep those individuals in mind as you bring your full intention to the following step.

The *fourth* step in letting go is forgiving anyone who has ever shown up as a star in your story, which includes forgiving yourself and anyone who has ever caused you to feel like a victim in any way. No matter how unsure you may be of your ability or willingness to do so, you will be capable of doing it once you embrace the fact that forgiveness is an *intention* rather than a reaction. Otherwise, unless you embrace it as an intention, you will likely perceive forgiveness as something you feel the need to justify. When in fact, it will ultimately serve you to simply forgive because you can—and then move on.

Still, it's critical to know that forgiving someone doesn't mean you are okay with what happened. You're granting forgiveness for the purpose of blessing both yourself and those who are willing to honor your intention with the gift of freedom.

The final step in letting go is to willfully declare your forgiveness into the universe by completing the *forgiveness process,* which you will find at the end of this chapter. I invite you to not only bring your full intention to doing so, but to allow the following teachings to shine a light on what's possible once you let things go.

Chapter 5 Teachings

5.1

As a result of what most of us were taught (or otherwise perceived to be true) as children, we are inclined to have bought into a vision for our future that causes us to still be living from the very same decisions we made back then.

In fact, given that our expectations for tomorrow tend to be shaped by whatever it is we're holding onto that caused yesterday to show up as it did, only by unleashing your full intention and giving yourself permission to think outside the past, will all that you dream of achieving finally becomes possible!

No matter how often you catch yourself lamenting yesterday, your history is *not* your destiny.

> "We are shaped by our thoughts; we become what we think. When the mind is pure, joy follows like a shadow that never leaves."
> —Buddha

In every moment, we are either inspired by what we perceive to be possible or dismayed by our belief in what isn't. Fortunately, we are fully in charge of what we believe. I invite you to believe in you.

5.2

We are either reinventing ourselves newly in every moment or living regurgitated versions of the past. In fact, given our inclination to gravitate toward the certainty of what we already know, unless we are intentionally showing up in alignment with our vision of what's possible, we're likely regurgitating by default. What's more, if you spend most of your time looking in your rearview mirror, you'll eventually crash and burn. Wisdom, therefore, if for those who intentionally focus on where they're going and not on where they've been.

> "Within each of us exists a power that is beyond our imagination. The ability to create an entirely new construct, from which we are free to create a completely different life. This is our birthright and is accessed by seeking the Truth."
> —Claudette Anderson

Are you living into a future being shaped by your intention and your purpose or are you settling for one that's being shaped by the stuff in your rearview mirror? Remember, even though you have a past, your past needn't have you.

5.3

Most of us tend to identify the major setbacks in our lives as the reasons we're not yet where we'd like to be, yet it's our beliefs about those setbacks that are truly holding us back and not the setbacks themselves.
Success, therefore, is for those who are quicker to challenge their beliefs than they are to declare war on their history. In other words, it's never about what you believe you're still dealing with that's keeping you stuck; it's what's between your ears…

"For one who has conquered the mind, the mind is
the best of friends. But for one who has failed to do
so, his very mind will be his greatest enemy."
—Bhagavad Gita

Freedom is for those who are forever willing to question what they believe about their pasts, as well as the ego that is doing the believing. Once you make friends with the truth, there's no reason to believe anything else.

5.4

Whenever you're feeling stuck or off purpose, I invite you to notice where you're making yourself or others wrong, and then be willing to give up doing so. No matter how uninspired we may feel at times, wisdom is for those who choose to live in alignment with their intention rather than how they feel, since our feelings are nothing more than proof that we are human.

In fact, once you replace making yourself and others wrong with *empathy,* and your fears with *faith,* all you'll feel from that moment on is unstoppable.

"Faith is a function of believing in something
before you have any reason at all to do so."
—Erica Nitti Becker

If ever you catch yourself lamenting anything at all, it will serve you to immediately shift your focus to something for which you are grateful. Should you be reminded of something for which you're not grateful, be grateful you survived it and then let it go.

5.5

No matter what we perceive to be standing in the way of our dreams coming true, it's rarely about what we're perceiving; it's about what we *believe* about what we're perceiving. For the most part, since the things we tend to believe are shaped by what we've always believed, we tend to be living lives that are little more than regurgitated versions of what didn't go well the first time around.

To break free from this trap, you must give yourself permission to dream bigger dreams and know that your past is simply where you *were* on the way to what you *deserve*.

Mastery is for those who focus forward and not backward.

> "Sometimes we stare so long at a door that is closing,
> that we see too late the one that is open."
> —Alexander Graham Bell

Where is anything you once believed to be true preventing you from being fully present to what's clearly true in the moment? No matter what you perceived to be true in the past, it will serve you to question how you came to believe it. Once you allow yourself to fall in love with where you're going, you'll have no reason to focus any energy at all on where you used to be.

5.6

Although most of us have suffered some form of indignity in the past, our minds don't retain the distinction of *being wounded*, they retain the memory of whatever we did that allowed us to survive whatever caused us to *perceive* that we were wounded, which it remembers as something we did wrong.

As a result, and in the wake of anything that leaves us feeling this way, all of us are inclined to make up a story about *how not good enough we are* instead of celebrating how resourceful we were to have survived it, which, unfortunately, is because we are more inclined to believe our made-up story than the truth.

What's more, although it's totally up to us which story we believe, biology causes us to embrace the one where we're not good enough, since we are forever on the lookout for proof this is true.

Fortunately, no matter what story your mind wants you to believe, it's fully within you to believe the story with you as the hero since this is the one that's true. Freedom is for those who do.

"Peace comes from within. Do not seek it without."
—Gautama Buddha

Joyfulness is for those who have made peace with life's imperfections, who have embraced their ability to create their own light, and who are forever shining it on everyone, including themselves.

5.7

Setbacks are only temporary unless we declare them to be failures (or otherwise blame ourselves for whatever went wrong). In other words, no matter what happened, whether you're holding onto it as proof that you're not good enough, or as a lesson, is always up to you.

In fact, we rarely get depressed because of whatever it was that went wrong; we get depressed because we continue to *lament* what went wrong.

Although it's impossible to live a life that's free of things going wrong, it's entirely possible to live a life that's free of lamenting them. Ultimately, lamenting serves no purpose other than to make you feel terrible. So, unless you enjoy feeling terrible, I invite you to give up lamenting.

"Throw off your worries when you throw off your clothes at night."
—Napoleon Bonaparte

Worrying causes your imagination to create things you don't want, so it will serve you to give up worrying altogether. Happiness is for those with the wisdom to count their blessings instead of their challenges and focus on where they're going instead of on where they've been.

5.8

For all intents and purposes, life is a process of *becoming* rather than arriving.

Mastery is a function of being willing to dance with whatever the universe has sent your way.

Therefore, expecting to show up at some magical place where you've achieved or resolved everything once and for all is both inherently unrealistic and a recipe for disappointment.

As satisfying as it is to have set your sights on an outcome and to have succeeded in achieving it, wisdom is for those who are just as quick to deny anything in their past the right to vote as they are to bring happiness along for the ride, rather than hoping it shows up once they get where they're going.

> "Joy is a function of embracing what's so. Change is never
> painful; only your resistance to change is painful."
> —Buddhist proverb

Freedom is for those who are willing to go with the flow—versus having to have things their way—and who have chosen to replace *searching for answers* with *living in the question.*

5.9

We have been blessed with the ability to reinvent ourselves newly in every moment, yet most of us remain enamored with the past; both because we survived whatever happened, and it meets our need for certainty.

Even so, if your intention is to be fully present in every moment, you'll want to immediately put an end to your love affair with your rearview mirror.

In fact, given how we tend to lament specific memories more than others, if you truly intend to overcome doubting yourself, you must refuse to look back on any reasons you believe you have for doing so. What's more, since every one of our limiting beliefs were born in the past, wisdom is for those who are willing to leave them there.

> "Let go of your cup filled with yesterday so that
> you may drink the glory of this moment."
> —Rumi

We all have a need to feel certain, but until you embrace your ability to bring certainty along for the ride, it will continue to elude you. Once you start bringing certainty with you wherever you go, you'll be able to give up trying to extract it from where you've been.

5.10

Regardless of your personal history, nothing in your past can rob you of your destiny—unless you allow it to.
In fact, there is no reason at all to grant anything in your rearview mirror the right to vote, since all that really matters is where you are right now and where you're going.
What's more, even if your life has been less than a joyride at times, the only thing that prevents you from living the life of your dreams is your resistance to making peace with where you've been.
Happiness, therefore, is for those who have already kissed their past *goodbye* and will soon be welcoming all that they're about to make happen with a giant kiss *hello*.

> "Don't judge each day by the harvest you reap
> but by the seeds that you plant."
> —Robert Louis Stevenson

If you spend most of your time contemplating worst-case scenarios, guess what's likely to show up? While it's certainly prudent to be mindful of anything you feel you need to avoid, you must never let anything rob you of your vision of what's possible. We get what we anticipate. Anticipate wisely.

5.11

Whether you already have a meaningful vision for your future and are moving in that direction—or are still trying to figure things out—patience is not only a virtue, its essential.

In fact, given that nowhere in nature does anything adapt or morph into something more magnificent overnight, if you fail to bring patience along for the ride, you'll find that it's taking you even longer to get where you want to go.

Remember, the caterpillar becomes the butterfly—but not before it's done being the caterpillar. Trust the process. Stay your course. Be patient.

> "The greatest thing is this world is not so much where
> we stand as in what direction we are moving."
> —Johann Wolfgang Von Goethe

Life is a treasure hunt, yet only by letting go of your belief that you know what treasure looks like will you not only be able to see the silver lining when things don't go your way, you'll be able to spin those silver linings into gold.

5.12

The first step toward believing you can, is to acknowledge that something in your past has likely hypnotized you into believing you can't. In fact, since all of us have either given up or rethought our plans more times than we can count, the path to anywhere worth going is bound to be littered with our own broken dreams.

No matter how often you've changed your mind in the face of an unexpected challenge, success is for those who are just as quick to ignore the litter as they are to step boldly into the future.

> "You've been criticizing yourself for years and it hasn't worked.
> Try approving of yourself and see what happens."
> —Louise L. Hay

The past is an illusion, so any fears or limiting beliefs that took root there are literally meaningless. Although there's no denying that the past is what's so; as it pertains to whatever you're committed to moving forward, it's also *so what*.

5.13

Our decisions shape our destiny, but since we have spent so much of our lives living at the mercy of our survival instincts, too many of our decisions were made with our heads planted firmly up our butts rather than with our full consideration. Whenever you catch yourself repeating the same silly mistakes, you are living in reaction to one or more unconscious decisions you made in the past, which are continuing to shape how you're showing up today.

Fortunately, once you take responsibility for having made those reactive decisions—while allowing for the fact that all of them were born of your inherent fear of not being good enough—you'll be inspired to override those decisions and show up *on purpose* instead. Mastery is for those who, even as they are willing take full ownership of any poor decisions they have made in the past, refuse to keep beating themselves up for having done so!

> "A man cannot be comfortable without his own approval."
> —Mark Twain

Disappointment is a function of focusing on what's missing. Passion is for those who are committed to focusing on what's possible and who refuse to settle for less. In other words, feeling passionate or disappointed is always a matter of choice. Choose wisely.

5.14

The good news is that we are survivors. In fact, if you hadn't survived everything you've had to endure, you wouldn't be here to celebrate this truth. You certainly deserve to pat yourself on the back for having done so, but if you allow your past to define your future, you'll likely remain blind to what's attainable moving forward.

Once you unleash your imagination and give yourself permission to think outside the past, all that you've ever dreamed of achieving instantly becomes possible.

Ultimately, no matter what you've had to overcome, success is a function of knowing that where you intend to go has nothing at all to do with where you've been.

> "We are shaped by our thoughts; we become what we think. When the mind is pure, joy follows like a shadow that never leaves."
> —Buddha

No matter where you've been or what you've been through, anything you envision as possible moving forward is fully achievable, and it's fully within you to make it happen. Any perceived exception to this truth is an illusion, so it will serve you to pay it no heed at all.

5.15

Being fully present in the moment doesn't mean you're any less committed to where you're going, but it does require that you refuse to live there until you do.

In fact, no matter how committed you are to self-improvement or to your vision moving forward, there will naturally exist a gap between where you are now and where you want to be.

What's more, if you focus more on where you're not (on the gap) than on where you want to be (your intention), you will likely continue to be disheartened and lose sight of who you truly are.

Joyfulness is for those who embrace and celebrate what *is* rather than worrying about what *isn't*.

> "Caught by our own thoughts, we worry about everything, but once we get drunk on love, whatever will be, will be."
> —Rumi Shahram Shiva

Mastery is for those who spend more time counting their blessings than they do lamenting what's missing. Wisdom is for those who count what they can see and not what they can't.

5.16

To be human is to have a fear of loss, which causes us to focus on certain memories more than others, which also gives rise to our very own private collection of limiting beliefs. Even though these beliefs tend to rob us of our passion, we're inclined to hold onto them because they provide us with certainty.

Unfortunately, our preoccupation with these beliefs causes us to remain married to what doesn't serve us, while preventing us from attracting what will.

Mastery, therefore, is for those who are both quick to let go of what was and even quicker to open their hearts to what's next.

In the end, only by being willing to terminate your love affair with your rearview mirror will you realize that you have nothing to lose—and you have everything to gain.

> "The birds always find their way to their nests. The river always finds its way to the ocean".
> —Zen proverb

Only by letting go of the need to have things your way (otherwise known as control) will you be inspired to access all the love in your heart and give it away. Freedom is for those who do.

5.17

The first step to achieving more than you've been achieving is to believe in more than you've been believing. Otherwise, the best way to *not* achieve what you want is to continue to believe that everything you think is true. In fact, since most of what we tend to believe is shaped by what we've always believed, most of us are living lives that are little more than regurgitated versions of where we've already been.

In support of breaking free of this trap, you must be willing to dream bigger dreams, but never forget that even though you have a past, your past needn't have you.

"We do not learn by experience, but by our capacity to experience."
—Gautama Buddha

Random thoughts are meaningless, so there's no reason to allow them to keep voting on your behalf. In other words, whether you allow what you're thinking to be shaped by something meaningless or meaningful is always up to you. Think wisely.

5.18

Wisdom is for those who have let go of the belief that something's missing and have come to know that whoever they wished they were, is who they already are.

As a function of being human, all of us have access to our very own private collection of less than pleasant memories of the past, which we're compelled to hold onto simply because we survived them. Even so, how we feel about these memories has nothing at all to do with what we had to endure; it has to do with the *story* we're telling ourselves about what we had to endure.

Mastery is for those who have left their old stories behind, knowing that forgiveness makes for a much better story. Freedom is for those who know that wherever they are right now is precisely where they're supposed to be.

"Forgive others not because they deserve forgiveness,
but because you deserve peace."
—Buddha

We are fully in charge of what we perceive to be possible in every moment. In fact, since any exception to this truth is an illusion, the entire world is your playground. Go play.

5.19

Even if your past has been a nightmare at times, it's still fully within you to create the life of your dreams. However, unless you're willing to make peace with where you've been, even when waking up to a day that appears to be unfolding like it did in your dreams, there's a pretty good chance that you're watching a rerun of one of your nightmares.

In fact, nowhere in your past are you likely to find any evidence that you're good enough since the only memories your mind is holding onto are the ones it's storing as proof that you're not.

Therefore, if your intention is to bring who you truly are to everything you're committed to, you need to look in your heart, rather than your memory.

"The best way to predict your future is to create it".
—Abraham Lincoln

Freedom is for those who are both willing to question what they believe about their past and *the mind* that's doing the believing. Once you teach your mind the truth, there's no reason for either of you to believe anything else.

5.20

As the creators of our lives, although we've all been blessed with the ability to reinvent ourselves newly in the moment, we tend to remain enamored with the past, simply because we survived it.

And yet, to be fully present *in the now,* you must not only be willing to give up your infatuation with where you've been, you need to put falling in love with where you're going at the top of your to-do list.

Joyfulness is for those who are quicker to focus on what's possible moving forward, than on where they used to be.

"I am not what happened to me; I am what I choose to become."
—Carl Jung

The only way to overcome your mind's inclination to look backward is to replace waking up thinking about who you've been with waking up looking forward to who you're becoming. All the joy imaginable is for those who do.

5.21

Given our inherent fear of not being good enough—as well as our inclination to focus on memories that tend to validate this fear—too many of us tend to wonder just "how good enough" we really are. And yet, since we're also inclined to grow even stronger in the wake of anything we've had to overcome, the more appropriate question would be: do you simply have a past—or does your past have you?

After all, if we were meant to focus on where we've been instead of on where we're going, we'd have been born with eyes in the back of our heads. Clearly, our destinies lie before us, yet since everything we focus on—as well as the meaning we attach to it—determines how we feel, would you rather focus on how poorly you feel in the wake of what you've been through, or on the hero you truly are for overcoming it?

Fortunately, although we have very little control over what's vying for our attention, we have *total control* over what we choose to focus on and the meaning we attach to it.

"To be wronged is nothing unless you remember it."
—Confucius

Whether you're living your life addicted to where you've been or excited about where you're going is totally up to you. I invite you to get high on where you're going.

5.22

Freedom is for those who are willing to make peace with the past by letting things go…

Clearly, if ever you've been abused or disrespected in any way, there's no justifying any such behavior—yet within each of us live the ability to separate the truth about what happened from the story we've likely been telling ourselves about it—especially to the extent that we feel diminished or damaged as a result.

Mastery, therefore, is a function of understanding that whatever happened was more about the perpetrator (and their role in their own story) than it was about you—and that it had nothing to do with your worthiness.

Forgiveness is never a sign that you condone whatever happened, it's an expression of your inherent power. Give yourself the gift of freedom. Let things go.

> "Hate is a monkey on your back. It weighs you down. Hate may be destroying your life. Meanwhile, the person you hate may not know or care. He or she may even be dead. Forgiving is a gift to yourself. You forgive so you can get on with your life."
> —Ron Potter-Efron

Never allow anyone who has hurt you to own you in any way. Accept whatever happened—and you will know peace. Let it go—and you will know freedom. Forgive it—and you will know love. Be grateful for it as the source of your strength—and you will know God.

Chapter 5 Key Concept

It's never your past setbacks or memories that are holding you back; it's what you *believe* about whatever happened that's holding you back.

> "The act of surrender and acceptance is the greatest force of subtle courage."
> —Dawn Harlow

The Forgiveness Process

What you'll need: a notebook to capture you notes, and a highlighter.

This exercise is about acknowledging your power as the creator of your life. In other words, your ability to choose to break free of anything you've been holding onto from the past. Ultimately, it's about forgiveness.

Most likely, any incident you've been unwilling or unable to forgive has been stored in a relatively prominent location within your "collection" (that place in your mind where you've been keeping track of all the proof that you aren't good enough).

However, whether you've been keeping track of any of these memories in a prominent manner or not, I assure you that any specific memory of anything you feel you need to forgive is being stored as proof that you're not good enough somewhere in your mind—so you'll have no trouble recalling it.

Again, if you suffered any form of abuse or disrespect, there is no way to justify this behavior. However, what is available when evaluating anything from this side of what you now know about letting go of the past is the ability to segregate *the truth* about what happened from *the story* you've likely been telling yourself about it, especially as it pertains to your role in that story.

> "Forgiveness in no way justifies the actions that caused your wounding, nor does it mean you have to seek out those who harmed you. It is simply a movement to release and ease your heart of the pain and hatred that binds it. It is the harvested fruit of a season of darkness, followed by a season of growth and of very hard work."
> —Dawna Markova

The first step in forgiving anyone for anything is to reevaluate the situation from what you now know after reading the previous five chapters. In almost all cases, any unwillingness or inability to let go or forgive is caused by the feeling that we aren't worthy of being forgiven ourselves (not being good enough), hence the unwillingness to forgive whoever caused our wounding in the first place.

However, now that you are aware of your ability to know yourself as whole, complete, and fully worthy, there is no reason to hold onto anything that suggests otherwise. In fact, I invite you to notice if you haven't already let go of some of the negative energy you once associated with some of these incidents from your past—and then allow that to inspire you moving forward.

The purpose of this exercise is to reevaluate any traumatic incident in your past where you've been unwilling or unable to forgive someone for causing you pain or sorrow, with the intention of discovering the truth. And, as we all know, the truth shall set you free.

To begin, please create the following heading in your notebook: To Be Forgiven.

First, identify any incidents from the past that you've been unable to forgive by writing down the name of the individual and a brief description of what happened.

Next, reflect upon each incident, one at a time, with the intent to determine when, during the incident, you decided you weren't good enough. Remember, this is an innate fear; thus, even when victimized by another, most of us tend to believe that if only we had been good enough, the incident wouldn't have occurred.

Notice that this incident delivered you directly into the place where you've been storing your collection of proof that you're not good enough, where you then made several decisions regarding this incident. Given which, whom did you blame for this incident, and what decisions did you make? No matter what you decided, notice that you had no control over these decisions.

In situations where you may have been abused or suffered a major indignity, in addition to the perpetrator, did you blame yourself or anyone else? If so, who?

Now, disassociate from this incident as best you can and assume the identity of an unbiased consultant. From this perspective, think back on this incident and notice whether the perpetrator was attempting to dominate anyone else or to avoid the domination of their life in general. Did they do what they did to win, to be right, or to prove that they were good enough, given their concern that they were not? In other words— and although this does not justify their actions—did the perpetrator act or react out of survival and/or their own inherent fear of not being good enough?

Continuing to observe this incident as a consultant, can you see that the victim (you) had no choice but to make the decisions they made or to feel how they've felt ever since? Can you now see that the ex-victim (you) deserves to no longer be held hostage by the pain of a situation over which they had no control? Can you further see that this situation had nothing to do with whether you are worthy? Expect to see these things—and you will. Allow for them because they are true.

Can you also see that even though you may have the right to be upset, there's absolutely no value in holding onto this incident or considering it proof of anything? Can you also see that this incident has been taking up far too much space and energy in your life? And are you finally willing to give it up forever?

If so, close your eyes and visualize whatever memoriam you earned for this incident crumbling into tiny pieces—and watch as the pieces disintegrate into dust—and then be empowered as this dust is blown away by the breath of the Divine Spirit.

Finally, go back to this list and overwrite each entry with the phrase: "I am worthy. I forgive." As you write these words, let go of any lingering negative emotion by allowing yourself to feel whatever empathy you can for whomever it is you need to forgive—as well for as yourself.

In the end, reflect truthfully on each incident to confirm that you are no longer feeling any leftover pain or anxiety.

Repeat this process for any incident you feel you haven't let go of completely. At this point, these incidents should exist for you as nothing more than simple truths. And while the truth is clearly *what's so,* it will serve you to embrace that fact that it's also *so what.*

"Forgiveness does not change the past, but it does enlarge the future."
—Paul Boese

CHAPTER 6

Vision and Passion

Showing Up as the Superstar
You Were Born to Be

Who have you envisioned yourself to be with respect to your future?

If you could make any dream or vision a reality, what would it be?

Who, besides you, would benefit as a result?

Remember, first you dream the dream—and then it comes true.

> "In order to carry a positive action, we must
> develop here a positive vision."
> —Dalai Lama

Since you would never show up in anything other than a joyful state on purpose, if ever you're not feeling joyful, you're obviously not living on purpose.

Question: What is your primary purpose behind reading this book? Is there anything specific you feel you have yet to master and are hoping to improve your chances of mastering it? Or are you still trying to figure out what mastery is all about?

In fact, unless you know exactly what you want and where you want to go, your chances of ending up where you want to be are slim. And yet, as important as it is for you to become clear about your vision and your purpose, it isn't so much about where you are right now, it's how determined you are and how you feel about where you're going that truly matters.

In every moment, how you feel and how you're showing up is tied directly to your intention, which is a virtual reflection of the degree to which you are truly living in alignment with your vision and your purpose. This, in turn, is tied to how much intentional energy you're bringing to what you're doing, and that's being fueled by how passionate you are about it all.

Whenever we are living intentionally and in alignment with flow, it's pretty much a toss-up as to whether we're feeling our passion because we're living on purpose, or is it because we're showing up on purpose that we tend to bring more passion to the party?

Although the answer is both, it's practically impossible for you to play full-out unless you're showing up in alignment with your vision. In other words, whether it's your passion that's the driving force behind your intention or your intention that's fueling your passion, the universe isn't likely to even notice unless you're doing it all in alignment with your ultimate purpose. And yet, how can you possibly show up *on purpose* if you don't even have one?

Energetically, the universe never responds to who you *think* you are; it responds to who you *believe* you are. So, unless you give yourself something grand enough to believe in, you'll continue to wander aimlessly among all the things vying for your attention, and even when you are feeling better, you'll still be inclined to feel like your life is *doing you* rather than feeling like you are in charge!

In fact, how can the universe respond to who you *believe* you are unless you're already showing up like it's who you already are? In other words, do you already know what you want (your vision), why you want it (your purpose), and then willfully show up this way even before you feel you've earned the right to do so? And even though this may feel like *faking it until you make it,* it's never a function of faking it; it's a function of creating it and owning it.

In fact, although there's nothing at all fake about honoring your passion more than your intellect, our very intention to show up in alignment with our ultimate vision actually requires that we pay no heed at all to our cultural conditioning—which wants us to believe that it wouldn't be right for us to show up *absolutely certain* unless we've already earned the right to do so; a dynamic most of us often call the "imposter syndrome", which causes us to feel like a fraud, unless we've already paid our dues, are at least hoping things work out, never stop trying, or are at least dutifully waiting for "someday" to arrive.

Breaking news! There is no luck, there is no hope, and there is no try. So, what the hell are you waiting for? In fact, if you truly intend to show up on purpose, you must bring "showing up" to the party—all the while knowing that this has nothing to do with being an imposter, but about refusing to keep your vision to yourself.

Still, as quick as the universe is to honor who you believe you are, it pays even more attention to what you're *doing*. Therefore, the only way it will ever put its money where your mouth is, depends upon you taking consistent action in the direction of what you intend to make happen!

However, it's not so much what you're doing that makes a difference; it's that you're doing it on purpose toward your *ultimate vision*. Otherwise, you will likely continue to show up as that blind squirrel who is simply hoping to find an acorn.

Figuring out your "why" always comes down to one very simple question: What specifically are you passionate about? To find out, simply take a few moments to reflect upon the following three questions. This will not only get your juices flowing, but the exercises at the end of this chapter will support you in delving even deeper into who you are and what you were put here to do.

1. Why are you here?
2. What do you want to achieve?
3. Who is going to benefit once you achieve it?

Even though mastery is about taking ownership of who you are and showing up in alignment with your vision, it's primarily a function of bringing nothing less than your full intention to everything you do.

In fact, you're never going to convince the universe that you're bringing your full intention to what you're doing by simply raising your game just enough to get by. Unless everything you're putting out there is inspired by a vision and a purpose grand enough to keep your mind from imploring you to give up, it likely won't be long until *it* does—and *you* do.

It's never about faking it until you make it; it's about *playing full-out* until you make it. In other words, it's about putting your vision out there—as well as putting your ass out there!

When it comes to making things happen, unless you truly know where you're going, how the hell are you going to get there? After all, even if you have a GPS, unless you tell it where you intend to go, it's simply going to tell you where you are.

No matter where you are, if you're truly committed to making your life a masterpiece, it's critical that you create an actual *life plan* that declares both your vision and your purpose to the universe—while also declaring how you intend to show up in support of making your personal vision a reality.

To which end, I invite you to allow the exercises in the following section to support you in becoming as clear as possible about your vision and your intention—while also creating an all-inclusive master plan for your entire life. This will ensure that everything you do in support of your vision is always on purpose.

Since waiting until later is for those who are less committed to achieving mastery than you are, to support you in getting started on the first section of your plan right now, you will find my personal *ultimate vision* and *ultimate purpose* statements below—which. I've included to allow you to get a head start on creating yours as soon as it serves you to do so. I further invite you to borrow any of my actual wording and allow yourself to enjoy the process.

Note: additional instructions for completing your vision and purpose statements, including your full-up Life Plan, are included in the section II exercises, following this chapter.

Ultimate Vision —Michael Nitti

To live intentionally and gratefully, always knowing that my life is a creation and that I have full power over what I say and how I am. To live, love, and interact with everyone else from the highest level of consciousness and to assume full responsibility for my every action. To awaken each day fully associated to the privilege of living my life in service to others and to seek out every opportunity to do so. To inspire, empower, cause great laughter, and lead others beyond their fears by continually stepping beyond mine. To raise the torch as high as possible—knowing that it is no brief candle—and to hand it off to as many as possible before I die.

<u>Ultimate Purpose </u>—Michael Nitti

To have more than my share of fun by living as if I were thirty-two for the rest of my life. To live freely, outrageously, and fully connected to my masculine core. To assume full responsibility for my personal transformation, knowing that it is a gift—and to share that gift with the intention of inspiring others to experience themselves as whole, complete, and magnificent. To love first, listen second, speak third—and always lead and speak from my vision. To be joyous, loving, and grateful and to fall into bed each night having inspired as many lives as possible before loving my wife to sleep.

Again, whether you take the time right now to create your own vision and purpose statements, keep in mind that the life-planning process is never about identifying every individual step you need to take in in support of achieving a specific outcome; it's about getting clear about where you're going and why.

To which end, and in support of everything you intend to make a reality, I invite you to allow the following teachings to shine a light on what's possible once this clarity shows up.

Chapter 6 Teachings

6.1

Vision without passion is like a car with no fuel. Vision without purpose is like a car with fuel, but no GPS or any specific place to go. In the absence of any specific place to go, there's no need for the car.
This being true, what is driving you right now? Are you okay with simply going through the motions—or are you in pursuit of something grand? As

you can imagine, a worthy purpose is a lot more likely to pull your butt out of bed. If you're not waking up on fire, you've either lost sight of your vision—or you haven't taken the time to invent a grand enough vision in the first place.

Passion is for those who are clear about who they are, what they want, and why they want it. In fact, only by falling in love with your why will the "how's" appear.

> "The two most important days of your life are the day
> you were born and the day you find out why."
> —Mark Twain

If you find yourself waiting to feel inspired before unleashing your passion, what, exactly, are you waiting for? Frankly, unless you're willing to show up with your passion in tow, why even show up?

6.2

The only reason any of us are reluctant to declare our visions publicly is for fear of looking foolish if things don't work out. And yet, by keeping your dreams to yourself, you are sending a message to the universe that you have little or no faith in what you're doing, so it will see no reason to send you what you need in support of what you intend to accomplish.

When it comes to making things happen, it's imperative that you are willing to put your dreams on loudspeaker and then refuse to put your feet up until they come true.

> "The reasonable man adapts himself to the world. The
> unreasonable man persists in adapting the world to himself.
> Therefore, all progress depends on the unreasonable man."
> —George Bernard Shaw

Leaders strive for excellence, not approval. Success is for those who spend more time doing what they know must be done than they do trying to prove to others that they know what they're doing.

6.3

The universe adores you and is totally aligned with your grandest, most heartfelt intentions. As for being enamored with your ego? Not so much. In fact, once you're living in full alignment with your vision and purpose, it will shine a light on your path and continue to send you all you need in support of making your dreams come true. On the other hand, if ever you decide to make it all about *you* at the expense of others, be prepared to go it alone.

> "Look in the Mirror and decide you are brave enough to live your life
> by staying true to your vision and not the expectations of others."
> —Loren Lahav

In the garden of life, when love is what you sow, love is what you reap. Even so, unless you tend to it daily, you'll find it overrun with weeds. Fortunately, by simply refusing to allow your ego to plant any seeds, you'll never have to contend with rotten fruit.

6.4

Whether you're conscious of it or not, every little thing you're leaving in your wake as the captain of your ship is either something you'll be happy to reflect upon later, or not. In every moment, how you're showing up and how you are treating others is forever up to you. By simply being aware of everything you're affixing your signature to—as you're creating it—your chances of being rewarded with more happy memories than regrets are clearly stacked in your favor.

On the other hand, since it's also up to you as to whether you're putting your signature on anything you'll be sorry for down the road, I invite you to never leave anything behind that you'll one day wish you hadn't.

> "If you want a certain thing, first be a certain person. Then
> obtaining that certain thing will no longer be a concern."
> —Zen proverb

We are either waiting for others to do something deserving of our love and support or giving it away freely simply because we can. Heaven is for those who see no reason to wait.

6.5

It has been said that when you give up your dreams, you die. Not so. It's when you stop listening to your heart that you die inside. In fact, when most of us are pursuing what we believe to be our dreams, what we're truly enamored with is the fruit. Then we get so caught up in chasing it, we too often fail to follow the path to becoming the tree that bears it.

To avoid this trap, I invite you to focus less on what you're chasing and more on what your heart is calling you to do. Only by becoming the tree and expressing your "tree-ness" as fully as possible into the universe will your actions ultimately bear the fruit you deserve.

Remember, the universe doesn't respond to dreams; it responds to how you're showing up and what you're putting out there.

> "Vision without execution is hallucination."
> —Thomas Edison

Joyfulness is for those who replace waking up wondering what they're going to get with waking up already knowing what they're going to give.

6.6

If ever you find yourself wondering what's next, although it will serve you to remain open to whatever the universe is sending your way, if anything shows up that doesn't seem to fit, perhaps it's not supposed to.

Trust your intuition. Clearly, none of us were meant to eat, drink, buy, or make love to everything that comes our way. Although the universe is forever sending us what we need, there's no reason to assume that we need everything it's sending. In every moment, how you choose to deal with everything flowing in your direction is always up to you. Deal wisely.

> "The birds always find their way to their nests. The
> river always finds its way to the ocean."
> —Zen proverb

You would never show up at the pick-up window of a drive-through without placing an order first—so why assume that everything that shows up on your doorstep was meant for you? In fact, when things show up that make no sense, it's okay to turn them away. Mastery is for those who refuse to take ownership of anything less than they deserve.

6.7

Happiness is an intention—not a destination. In fact, given that we are fully in charge of how we're showing up in every moment, it's clearly up to us to bring our full intention along for the ride, no matter where it is we're going. The only way unhappiness can hitch a ride is if we forget that we're in charge.

Once you take ownership of your ability to live on purpose, you'll realize that happiness isn't a feeling you go to a party in search of; it's an intention you *bring* to the party.

> "I am happy and content because I think I am."
> —Alain Rene Lesage

Wisdom is for those who would never show up at a party *hoping* to have a good time unless they've already brought an intention to have a good time to the party. Passion—don't leave home without it.

6.8

Joy is a function of spending more time looking to make a difference than you do looking for proof of your worthiness. Frankly, we were born worthy, yet in the absence of an intention to contribute beyond ourselves, we tend to wait for something beyond our own creation to inspire us to feel our passion. Since passion is who you already are, if you keep waiting for it to show up, you'll likely be waiting a long damn time.

Mastery is for those who have given up the wait and chosen to shine their light as brightly as they can in support of making the incredible difference they were born to make.

> "The future has several names; for the weak, it is impossible. For the fainthearted, it is unknown. For the valiant, it is ideal."
> —Victor Hugo

Unless you're speaking passionately and from your heart, anything you're saying is showing up as hot air. Frankly, the planet doesn't need more hot air, so do us all a favor—find your passion.

6.9

No matter how smart we think we are, in the absence of a truly inspiring dream or an equally compelling intention, we have nothing. In fact, unless you are consciously showing up on purpose and in alignment with your vision, you are, by default, living in reaction.

Although the lack of a stated purpose may provide the illusion of freedom— no pressure, no fear of failure, and no responsibility—you will never break free from your little voice wondering if this all there is? Fortunately—and no matter what your mind is whispering in your ear—all of us were born with the innate ability to bring our passion with us wherever we go.

Mastery, therefore, is for those who *bring it all* and ensure that whatever they do with whatever they bring is whatever it takes to make their dreams come true!

> "There is no more liberating, no more exhilarating experience than to determine one's position, state it bravely, and then to act boldly."
> —Eleanor Roosevelt

Are you passionately pursuing all that you want to make happen—or waiting for what you want to find you? Once you refuse to go anywhere without your passion in tow, the universe will be inspired to send you what you need, and all that you refuse to live without right along with it!

6.10

If you sit around waiting for your dreams to come true, the only thing you'll ever achieve is the realization that they didn't come true while you were sitting around waiting. In fact, action (born of intention) is both the fuel and the fire that inspires us to step beyond the mundaneness of simply allowing our lives to unfold as they may.

Mastery, therefore, is for those who refuse to wait and who allow their creativity to inspire what they're doing rather than simply surrendering to the unfolding.

Remember, your fears aren't going to die until you do, so if you're waiting for them to stop questioning what you're up to, you'll be waiting a long damn time.

> "A man who waits to believe in taking action before
> he does so is anything you like, but he's not a man
> of action. You must act as you breathe."
> —Georges Clemenceau

> "You have always had the power, my dear; you
> just had to learn it for yourself."
> —Glinda the Good Witch

You have always had access to the full measure of your intentionality, my dear. You simply had to set it free!

6.11

When it comes to creating the life of your dreams, it's been said that persistence is the key to success. And yet, if you're still trying to figure out where you're going, persistence may result in you digging yourself a very deep hole rather quickly.

In consideration of this possibility, it's critical that you at least get clear about your outcome—even if you're not yet clear about your *how.*

Although fire-fire-aim will get you out of the gate and immediately into the game, success is for those who are clear about where they want to end up before they shift the throttle to full speed ahead.

"If someone is going down the wrong road, he doesn't need motivation to speed him up. What he needs is education to turn him around."
—Jim Rohn

If ever you feel you've lost your way, only by admitting that you have no clue, will the universe finally start sending you clues. In fact, the surest way to remain clueless is to *act* like you know where you're going rather than asking for directions. Wisdom is for those who replace acting with *asking.*

6.12

Most of us have yet to declare our true purpose in life either because we've yet to find one or because we're still waiting for it to reveal itself. Unfortunately, not only is waiting for your purpose to show up a terrible idea; unless and until you discover your *why*, you'll never achieve your *what.*

Success, therefore, is for those who are no less committed to turning waiting into action than they are to refusing to put up their feet until everything they want shows up at their door.

Passion is a function of looking into your heart, making friends with what you find there, and then refusing to settle for anything less than you deserve.

"The noblest pleasure is in the joy of understanding."
—Leonardo da Vinci

Self-improvement is a grand pursuit—but only when you're intending that it move you from good to great and not unworthy to worthy. Once you embrace your inherent worthiness, your purpose will find you.

6.13

Whether you're open to what it's sending you or not, the universe is forever acting in alignment with your vision, which is why it's critical that you have one and that you're living from it.

Do you believe that you're currently taking full advantage of everything that's flowing in your direction—or are you waiting for clarity? Only by taking meaningful action in the direction of your dreams will the clarity you've been waiting for be inclined to show up. At which point, only by continuing to stay your course, will you ultimately come to realize that everything is unfolding as it should. Remember, first *you* show up—and then things show up.

Even as you stand in the clarity of what's unfolding, only by refusing to be denied will all that you desire and deserve find you.

> "The greatest danger for most of us is not that our aim is too
> high and we miss it, but that it is too low and we reach it."
> —Michelangelo

If you allow yourself to be okay with settling for what you need instead of pursuing what you want, the universe will simply send you what you need. However, by simply upping your intention—while refusing to settle for less—all that you've ever wanted will be yours.

6.14

Energetically, anything we can envision is possible, yet most of us spend more time hoping this is true than we do knowing that if we can dream it, we can create it. Visualizing your dreams coming true is the secret sauce that enables us to move beyond simply hoping things work out, as well as the intention that inspires us to stay our course until what we want shows up.

Success, therefore, is for those who allow their vision to be the driving force behind every action they take and the energy behind their intention to never give up!

"Men do not quit playing because they grow old;
the grow old because they quit playing."
—Oliver Wendell Holmes

Life is a treasure hunt, yet only by letting go of what you expect it to look like will you be able to see the treasure in every little thing.

6.15

Success is a function of refusing to mistake activity for effective action. If you truly intend to succeed, you must devote more time to actively making things happen than you do to *getting ready* to make things happen. Leaders are those who have learned that in order for results to show up, they must show up first.

At the end of the day, once you stop worrying about how you're showing up and focus all of your positive intention on who you're being and where you're going, you'll show up just fine.

"A positive attitude may not solve all your problems, but it will annoy enough people to make it worth the effort."
—Herm Albright

Are you pursuing all that you deserve or waiting to be inspired? Inspiration has nothing to do with waiting and everything to do with doing what lights you up. I invite you to do just that.

6.16

The secret to overriding your reactive mind is to spend more time looking to serve and inspire others than you do looking for proof that you have what it takes to do so. In fact, since we were born with what it takes, there's no reason to be looking for anything other than opportunities to shine your light as brightly as you can.

Still, in the absence of intentionally showing up this way, it's not unusual for us to feel lost whenever we feel like we're not making a difference.

Fortunately, by simply shifting your focus from what's in it for you to what's in it for others, you'll instantly be introduced to the incredible difference maker you were born to be.

> "Don't judge each day by the harvest you
> reap but by the seeds you plant."
> —Robert Louis Stevenson

Mastery is never about finding what's missing or becoming something you're not; it's about letting go of whatever's been stopping you from unleashing who you already are into the universe.

6.17

Although patience is a virtue, putting off doing what you know must be done has nothing to do with patience. Putting things off is a function of fear. Energetically, patience is the ability to embrace delayed gratification only after you are actively engaged in the pursuit of what you desire. The only thing it will ever serve you to put on the back burner is fear itself (while moving your dreams to the front burner).

In fact, given that it's normal to have second thoughts when we're in pursuit of something grand, patience will allow you stay your course when your mind is screaming at you not to.

At the end of the day, success is for those with the wisdom to bring their vision along for the ride and who put their fears on hold rather than their dreams.

> "I am not defined by what someone has told me I
> can or cannot do. I am defined by the choices I make
> inside of who I say I am committed to being."
> —Faith Gorski

Are you focusing on what you want or on what's preventing you from having it? Are you being how you need to be and doing what you need to do in order to deserve and achieve it? No matter how committed you are to what you're committed to, you must show up first.

6.18

The surest way to undermine any dream or intention is to assume you're on the road to success, when in fact, you're actually glued to the path of least resistance. Your destiny will never show up on its own, so unless you truly expect your dreams to come true, the only thing you'll ever achieve is the realization that they didn't come true while you were glued to the wrong path.

Although there's certainly nothing wrong with taking the easier path to wherever you want to go, success is for those who take the "right" path.

> "The harder the struggle, the more glorious the triumph-
> self-realization demands very great struggle."
> —Swami Sivananda

The chances of stumbling upon anything of value while simply hoping your dreams come true are about the same as winning the lottery without buying a ticket. Success is for those who choose to wake up on fire and then begin each day by eating obstacles for breakfast before blazing trails of their own.

6.19

In the absence of a big enough reason to pull ourselves out of bed each day, most of us tend to arrive on time to wherever we're going for no other reason than to avoid being late. In other words, it's rarely our intention that inspires our promptness; it is our inclination to show up simply because we have to.

Stop the insanity! Although choosing not to declare a meaningful purpose may provide you with the illusion of freedom—no pressure, no fear of failure, and no responsibility—unless you say no to the illusion, you'll spend the rest of your life wondering how things might have turned out if you had said yes to what could have been.

No matter what you're avoiding or why, each of us was born with the ability to bring our full intention to everything we do. If you're not being fueled by your passion, you're being held hostage by the lack of it. Unless you're a fan of being held hostage, it will serve you to find your purpose.

> "You are either directing your own movie or playing a role in someone else's. You create, promote, or allow everything in your life."
> —Frank Clark

Although we all feel stuck at times, it's rarely for a lack of desire; it's for the lack of a compelling reason to step up. Once you find your purpose and passion, determination will find you.

6.20

Are you consciously making your own decisions—or are they making you? As a function of being human, it's literally impossible for us to avoid making decisions, for even if you decide to put things off, you've still made a conscious decision to put things off.

In other words, even if you think you have, you can never take yourself out of the equation.

Mastery, therefore, is for those who take full responsibility for everything they say, who speak directly from their heart, and who make every one of their decisions *on purpose*.

> "The heart of a fool is in his mouth, but the mouth of a wise man is in his heart."
> —Benjamin Franklin

Walking around with your head up your ass is no less of a lousy idea than it is a lousy strategy for success. Results are for those who refuse to speak from anywhere other than their heart and who stay the course even when their minds are pleading with them not to.

6.21

Life is fired at us point-blank. And although the ability to stay our course as we're being fired upon is always ours for the taking, it's available solely to those who refuse to get sucked into reaction by every little thing that doesn't serve them.

Given which, only by paying no attention at all to your reactive mind will the universe get the message that you have absolutely no intention of settling for anything less than taking full ownership of your power.

Mastery, therefore, is for those who are as quick to *say yes* to celebrating life as the treasure hunt that it is as they are to *say no* to anything that would prevent them from seeing the treasure in every little thing.

> "Vison without action is a daydream. Action
> without vision is a nightmare."
> —Japanese proverb

If you're okay with waiting for what you want to find you, the only thing you'll discover is that it didn't find you while you were sitting around waiting. Unless you refuse to wait for what you want to show up, you'll likely be waiting forever.

6.22

Success is for those who spend more time focusing on what they want and how to achieve it than they do worrying about how to explain things if they fail. In the face of any challenge, whether you're committed to making progress or excuses is always up to you.

Whenever things get tough, mastery is for those who know that any detours they encounter along the way are simply the universe's way of teaching them something they wouldn't have otherwise learned. It is not an indication that they should rethink their plans.

No matter what you're up against, the only way to overcome it is to dance with the detours, stay your course, and never give up.

> "To the person who does not know where he
> wants to go there is no favorable wind."
> —Seneca

You can't live a life free of making mistakes, but you can live a life free of repeating them. Mastery is for those who collect lessons and not regrets.

6.23

In the absence of a sincere intention to speak directly from the heart, it's totally normal for us to let our egos do our talking. And when we do, even though others may initially wonder where we're coming from—given that both energies tend to be expressed with a high degree of conviction—they'll surely figure it out soon enough.

The difference, of course, has to do with whether what you're saying is flowing *out* of you (from your need to prove or justify something) or flowing *through* you (in alignment with your intention to serve).

In every moment, whether you're committed to making a difference or a good impression is always up to you.

Mastery is for those who are forever shining their light on others rather than themselves.

> "Could a greater miracle exist than for us to look
> through each other's eyes for an instant?"
> —Henry David Thoreau

Whenever your intention is to make a difference instead of a good impression, you'll likely find that you're making a good impression anyway. Remember, the ego is insatiable, so feeding it actually leaves you hungry for the truth. Magic shows up when what you're saying is flowing out of your heart and not out of your ass.

6.24

A fool and his money are soon parted, yet if you live your life avoiding every situation where you might appear foolish, you'll likely never create enough wealth for this to be a concern. Prosperity is for those who have a higher regard for their ability to create all the abundance they deserve than they do for what others might think if they don't.

Although you'll probably never get rich acting like a fool, it is no less likely to happen if you spend every waking moment worrying about looking like one.

> "Daring ideas are like chessmen moved forward. They may
> be beaten, but they just may start a winning game."
> —Johann Wolfgang von Goethe

Although success is for those who allow their vision to be their guide, you'll never achieve all that you foresee yourself achieving unless you bring common sense along for the ride.

6.25

If ever you're having trouble staying your course, it's likely because you've lost sight of your purpose.

If so, the quickest way to reclaim your motivation is to ensure that you're shining your light on why you are here and what you're committed to—and not on the things you perceive to be standing in your way.

Success, therefore, is for those who focus on what's real and present in the moment and refuse to worry about every little thing that could go wrong. In fact, no matter what's vying for your attention, where you focus your *intention* is always up to you.

> "The only person you are destined to become
> is the person you decide to be."
> —Ralph Waldo Emerson

Whatever you intend to accomplish, although a desire to succeed is a good start, an unwillingness to fail is much more likely to pull your butt out of bed on fire. If you're truly committed to an outcome, you must be unwilling not to achieve it.

6.26

No matter how committed you are to a specific outcome, unless you're listening to your heart—rather than to your ego—it won't be long before everyone else wishes you had.

Mastery is for those who are totally clear about their why, and they are forever expressing it as passionately as possible to the universe. In fact, if you're putting anything other than your why out there, it's likely being received as you making stuff up. And since the last thing any of us need is your stuff, never leave home without your *why*.

> "When you express yourself with authenticity and
> passion you are speaking from your purpose."
> —Erica Nitti Becker

Since you would never play less than full-out on purpose, if you're not playing full-out, you're not living on purpose. Joy is for those who have found their why and never stop living from it.

6.27

Sadly, too many of us are inclined to withhold the full measure of our aliveness for fear of looking foolish.

Joyfulness is for those who refuse to bring anything less than the full measure of their passion to everything they do—so only by being willing to accept that something in your past has left you with a broomstick inserted firmly up your ass, will you discover how incredible you'll feel once you're willing to leave your past and the broomstick behind.

After all, nowhere is it written that toned down is the appropriate way to live one's life—yet unless you refuse to remove the broomstick, you'll spend the rest of your life having to choose between "being appropriate" and playing full-out.

At the end of the day, there is no *enlightenment* without *lighten*—so it will serve you to throw yourself a broomstick-burning party and lighten the hell up.

> "Find out where joy resides and give it a voice far beyond singing. For to miss the joy is to miss all."
> —Robert Lewis Stevenson

The greatest gift you can give others is the gift of your full self-expression. Joy is for those whose desire to share their passion with the universe is greater than their reasons not to.

6.28

Your power is in no way tied to the ebb and flow of forces beyond yourself. Even so, might a sudden shift in circumstances steer you in a different direction? Perhaps, yet it's fully within each of us to remain focused on our destination no matter the nature of any detour that may require us to adjust our course.

Remember, whether you're feeling like a puppet or committed to being the puppeteer is always up to you.

Once you are living in alignment with your vision, you'll realize it's you that's in charge of your own strings. Quit pretending that you're not.

> "We first make our habits and then our habits make us."
> —John Dryden

The first step toward discovering who you are is to acknowledge that you've been hypnotized into accepting who you are not.

6.29

> "To be yourself in a world that is constantly trying to make
> you something else is the greatest accomplishment."
> —Ralph Waldo Emerson

Even though all of us were born with the ability to dream bigger dreams, no one has ever popped out of the womb with a meaningful vision, since the default vision of our survival mind is to simply deliver us as safely as possible to wherever it wants us to go.

Therefore, unless you're more committed to listening to your mind than you are to unleashing your inner eagle, it will serve you to come up with something significantly more worthy of your intention. After all, why settle for survival when you were born to fly?

> "Most of us tiptoe through life in order to make it safely to death."
> —Theodore Roosevelt

Life is a treasure hunt, yet unless you refuse to let your mind do your hunting for you, you'll have no right to expect anything more of tomorrow than to wake up another day older.

Chapter 6 Key Concept

It's not that you don't know what you want or how to show up at a level 10; it's that you have not yet declared that you can. You must pursue life! Mastery is for those who live on purpose, with passion, and in pursuit of their vision, each and every day!

> "Your vision will become clear only when
> you can look into your own heart.
> Who looks outside, dreams; who looks inside, awakens."
> —Carl Jung

Section II Exercises
Turning Freedom into Action

Overriding your limiting beliefs. Stepping beyond whatever is keeping those beliefs in place. Declaring your Vision and Purpose in support of making your dreams come true, including how to forgive yourself and others.

1. What memories from your past are keeping you from taking action today?
2. What beliefs about yourself prevent you from taking action toward your goals?
3. What beliefs do you need to create in order to replace 1 and 2 above (and then live from them)?
4. What beliefs do you need to create in order to pursue the life of your dreams? How do you intend to remind yourself to show up this way?
5. Create your purpose and vision statements. Make them worth getting out of bed for!

(refer to Michael's examples earlier in this chapter, and see Erica's below).

Ultimate Purpose —Erica Nitti Becker

To inspire others to live their best lives by disregarding their mind telling them they can't or that the whole world is against them. To connect people to their inherent certainty, knowing that the past doesn't matter— and it will never serve them to worry about the future. To awaken their true desire for the purpose of turning it into reality. To help others pay more attention to the good in their lives, knowing that the bad is only as bad as they allow it to be—and that their inner strength is stronger than they ever knew.

To be a bright light for everyone in my life—a light that helps them find their own light, that they will then be empowered to shine on everyone else.

Michael A. Nitti, Erica Nitti Becker

Ultimate Vision —Erica Nitti Becker

To look back on a life that was fully aligned, fully present, and one of inspired action. To know that no matter how afraid I was, I took at least one step. To be grateful every day, especially for the opportunity to have been a part of someone's life. To know that I helped make the lives of others more conscious and fulfilling, and that I inspired them to be more energized in the pursuit of their dreams. To live abundantly, freely, and passionately—every single day!

In support of you in creating a full-up life plan based upon your purpose and vision statements, and to walk you step-by-step through this process, please visit www.distinctionsofmastery.com

"If you don't design your own life plan, chances
are you'll fall into someone else's plan.
And guess what they have planned for you? Not much."
—Jim Rohn

SECTION III

Stepping into Mastery

Taking full responsibility for each day, including what you focus on, how you feel, and your intention to show up as the superstar you were born to be. By the end of this section, you will be unwilling to bring anything less than all you've got to the party.

IV.   Ownership and Courage; The Truth of the Power flowing through you
V.   Excellence and Playing Full-Out; Bringing All You've Got to All You Do
VI.   Gratitude and Abundance; Saying No to Scarcity

Exercises: Turning Passion into Action
You are the designer of your life. Discovering that it's fully within your power to create the life of your dreams by overriding anything that's preventing you from doing so.

CHAPTER 7

Ownership and Courage

The Truth of the Power Flowing Through You

What is your greatest fear?

How much courage are you currently bringing to what you intend to create? What are you willing to commit to achieving right now?

> "Courage is knowing what not to fear."
> —Plato

Mastery is for those with the wisdom to bring courage along for the ride rather than waiting for it to show up on its own. No matter what you intend to accomplish, the first step in making any dream or goal a reality has nothing at all to do with trying to figure out *how* to achieve it; it's about being totally honest about what it is that's preventing you from doing so.

You see, even if your path appears to be overflowing with obstacles, I assure you that there is only one thing that ever stops any of us from achieving our goals: *fear.*

And although you may believe that what you're seeing is something other than fear, this is simply because chief among your mind's many other talents, is *master of disguise,* which is why we often refer to the things we see in our way by some other name, such as procrastination, prudence, confusion, lack of motivation, uncertainty, or even PTSD.

No matter what you've been calling it, your mind's job is to be on the lookout for anything it perceives as a threat to your success. In fact, whenever it detects even the slightest chance that you might fail (or otherwise appear foolish), it instantly springs into action, deploying its most trusted tool in steering you clear of any situation wherein your ego might take a hit. And no matter what your *master of disguise* has been calling it, that tool is fear.

Therefore, even if it's simply suggesting you rethink your plans, your mind is always on the hunt for your least risky option. And even though it's in no way opposed to your success, it *is* opposed to you falling short and being reminded (falsely of course) that you're not good enough.

Which is why your mind can pretty much be counted on to beg you to reconsider moving forward anytime it feels there's even the slightest chance of things not going your way.

Given that your mind will stop at nothing to prevent you from looking like you have no clue, the first step in overcoming any of your mind's disguises is to know that no matter what you feel is stopping you, it's in no way personal to you. And although it may feel personal, this is simply because this entire "perception-reaction" dynamic is linked directly to your inherent fear of not being good enough, which—as you now know—is something we all have in common.

For this reason, instead of setting a goal and then worrying about achieving it, it's often easier for you to listen to our mind and give up right away rather than chasing what you want a little farther down the road—only to give up later.

In the presence of all this temptation to give up—yet knowing that your master of disguise will be hosting this little game show of his forever—what's the secret to being able to decline all his invitations? No matter how relentless your mind has been at inviting you to all his "you're not good enough" parties, the first step is to know that it's totally normal for you to feel this way. No matter what disguise he's wearing, it's never proof that you should give up; it's simply proof that your survival instinct has kicked in. Then, knowing that any lingering second thoughts are merely your game show host doing his job, step boldly beyond your instincts, fully into your power, and never, ever give up!

What's more, now that you've created a life plan, I invite you to start showing up as who you have declared yourself to be and to immediately focus on whatever you want to create right now—all the while allowing the power of your intention to be your partner in overriding your mind when it's imploring you not to. No matter what your mind would have you believe, once your intention is bigger than your fear, you will act.

Courage and Supreme Certainty

Courage isn't the absence of fear; it is the energy that allows you to honor your vision more than your instincts and your intention more than your limiting beliefs. As you now know, your limiting beliefs are simply a bunch of lies your mind made up to keep you small and safe.

Mastery is refusing to entertain the lies and knowing that the ability to show up in a state of absolute certainty is already within you, simply waiting for you to access your intention and courage to set it free. In support of which, what's available to you right now is the ability to take full ownership of the following five key elements of absolute certainty, which are the keys to unlocking your full intention and courage. That's where all the magic happens.

1) Knowing yourself as the creator of your life. In other words, fully embracing your ability to step into a supremely certain state at will, knowing that embracing your full power needn't in any way detract from your intention to remain humble and respectful of others, and leaving everyone you meet equally willing to embrace their ability to show up in a fully certain state as well, inspired by your intention.

Still, as well intended as we may be in not wanting to appear too full of ourselves, we often end up throwing the baby out with the bathwater by unwittingly denying ourselves access to the fullest measure of our intentionality. However, since supreme certainty is an intention and shares no common energy at all with ego, we have every ability to show up as fully certain and fully supportive of others.

2) Knowing that even if you have a history of playing small or feeling less than fully certain at times, it is never proof that you're in any way devoid of the ability to show up this way. It is proof that you simply never knew you had this ability. In fact, this is how you've come to know pretty much everything you now know to be true, having been unaware of a specific truth right up until that *aha moment* when you finally came to know it. Something, in fact, that is likely true of many of the distinctions you've learned over the last six chapters, which are simply proof that you didn't know any of these things until you did—and now you do.

Again, it's never about trying to show up as anything that you're afraid you're not; it's about giving yourself permission to show up as the fully capable and competent difference maker you were born to be, which you likely would have been all along had your mind not built you a giant collection of limiting beliefs. Beliefs that have been robbing you of your certainty and your power, yet you've never known why.

Even though you now know what you didn't know, showing up in a state of absolute certainty is never a function of figuring out *how;* it's a function of finally embracing your ability to show up this way simply because you can. In other words, supreme certainty isn't simply who you are; it's who you've always been.

3) Being willing to dismiss the belief that you're a fraud whenever you're showing up as fully certain, yet in the absence of any specific evidence that it's warranted. In other words, refusing to listen to your little voice screaming, "Imposter!" in your ear—which is simply a tool your mind uses to keep you from showing up as too full of yourself. In fact, showing up in a fully certain state—simply because you say so—*really is* who you really are, and it has nothing to do with pretending or showing off.

After all, the ability to show up in a fully certain state isn't even a skill at all; it's an intention and a mindset. However, since we're inclined to perceive it as a skill, we tend to believe that our only hope is to acquire it over time—which is one of our most disempowering beliefs because it robs us of the ability to simply step into our power on demand. The only thing that can really stop any of us from showing up "on demand" is the belief that it's not already within us to do so—which, of course, it is.

4) Understanding that accessing your ability to show up in a fully certain state has nothing to do with knowing *how* to do so—but with being willing to give up the belief that you need to know how in the first place.

Again, all of us have been taught to believe that we need to attain a certain degree of knowledge in order to master a specific skill. And, with respect to an actual skill, that really is true. However, since showing up in a fully certain state is not a skill, but an intention, accessing it has nothing to do with knowing how; it's about believing that it's already within you to do so.

5) Giving up the belief that confidence is something that can only be built over time. Again, supreme certainty is neither a skill nor a belief, which is why figuring out how to show up in a supremely certain state is never a result of anything that can be learned. It is an intention that all of us are equipped to bring forth simply because we have it within us to do so.

Although you likely will feel more empowered the more you bring supreme certainty to the party, it's just as critical to know that since it's never a function of it showing up on its own, it's imperative that you refuse to go anywhere without intentionally bringing it along for the ride. In other words, you must refuse to leave home without it.

I invite you to allow the following teachings to shine a light on what's possible once you replace *waiting* for certainty and courage to show up with bringing both of them with you wherever you go!

Chapter 7 Teachings

7.1

No matter why you believe your dreams aren't coming true, wouldn't you prefer to have what you want rather than the reasons you don't? To override your reasons—otherwise known as limiting beliefs—it's imperative that you stop believing in them more than you believe in yourself.
Fear—disguised as reasons—is what's really stopping you, when all that's really missing is courage. Once you unleash your courage—which is already within you—all your reasons will magically disappear—and the freedom to do what you were put here to do will magically appear!

"It is not because things are difficult that we do not dare.
It is because we do not dare that they are difficult."
—Seneca

It's impossible to live a life that's free of making mistakes, but you can live a life that's free of repeating them. Mastery is for those who collect lessons instead of regrets and then spin those lessons into gold.

7.2

You can never outthink fear; you can only outdo it. There are no results tied to thinking—only doing.

In fact, that thing you've been calling procrastination is really nothing more than fear in sheep's clothing, all the while robbing you of your aliveness and your success.

No matter what you're up to, unless you're willing to leave your thinking cap and your sheep suit in the closet—and then refuse to leave home without your superhero undies—you'll never put an end to the thievery.

"Everything you want is just outside your comfort zone, one baby
step of courage at a time. The universe rewards the brave."
—Michelle Sorro

Fear wears many disguises, including procrastination, confusion, and laziness—none of which are flattering. Courage, however, looks great on everyone. Why not dress to win?

7.3

Although we tend to identify the obstacles we perceive to be standing between where we are now and where we want to be as huge and scary, it's really our minds that are huge and scary and most often in the way. In fact, since our inclination to live in reaction to our fears is simply the survival mind doing its job, it's totally normal for us to second-guess ourselves as often as we do.

Since there's absolutely no magic at all to be found in normal, only by unleashing your inner magician will you be inspired to conjure up enough courage to make your fears disappear. Once you marry your *inner magician* to your *inner warrior* and allow them to join forces, it's over.

"He who is not every day conquering some fear
has not learned the secret of life."
—Ralph Waldo Emerson

We are all seekers of the same joy, and we all feel the same fears. Within each of us resides a level of strength far beyond that of our own creation— as well as the ability to access it at will by simply embracing our oneness with the universe—versus the illusion that we're going it alone.

7.4

More often than not, lowered expectations are the result of a lowered sense of self, which, paradoxically, is an outgrowth of lowered expectations. On the ship of life, you are the captain of your fate. Even so, unless and until you declare yourself the captain, you'll be inclined to show up as just another passenger—resigned to simply hoping that your ship will come in. News flash! Hope is not a strategy for success, and no one is going to turn over control of the ship to a passenger. At the end of the day, unless you're okay with simply going along for the ride, it will serve you to step up and take command of your ship.

"My vision excites me. My passion invigorates me. Playing
full-out every day scares me. And that's how I know I
am fully alive and reaching my full potential."
—Erica Nitti Becker

Motivation is a function of devoting more energy to making your dreams come true than you do to dreaming itself. Devote wisely.

7.5

Although a steady diet of reflecting upon one's fears has never made anyone's top-ten list of strategies for success, courage truly is the breakfast of champions.

What's more, no matter what it is you're looking to accomplish, unless courage is the driving force behind everything you say and do, you're leaving way too much to chance.

However, once you allow intention to pull you out of bed and begin your day with a bowl of courage, all that you ever wanted will be yours!

"He who conquers others is strong. He who conquers himself is mighty."
—Zen proverb

Whether you're living your life addicted to excuses or to results is totally up to you. Mastery is for those who get high on courage.

7.6

It has been said that knowledge is the key to having it all. And yet, if you truly expect your dreams to come true, only by marrying your intellect to your true self will you gain access to who you really are—as well as a never-ending supply of courage. Actually, living the dream has very little to do with applying what you know and everything to do with how you're showing up while applying what you know.

In fact, no matter how clear you are about what you want to become, you'll never fully master your craft until you own it and are willing to declare it to be so. Ultimately, the key to mastering anything is to know that all you'll ever become is a function of who you declare yourself to be.

"What does it cost you to let your gifts go unacknowledged?"
—Madeleine Homan Blanchard

You are in charge of how much intention and courage you bring to the party at any given moment. Any perceived exception to this truth is an illusion. Knowing this is all you really need to know.

7.7

Unless you spend all of your time living under a rock, there will be times when you feel fear. And when you do, although your natural inclination would be to rethink everything you're committed to, what will truly save the day is love. In fact, love is the energy from which we are intuitively able to override our instincts by choosing to honor *that* which is flowing through us more than we honor our ego and our fears.

Ultimately, no matter what you're afraid of, when you speak and act from your heart, you gain access to a level of strength that is otherwise unattainable.

In the face of any challenge, meet it with compassion, and courage will soon follow.

"From caring comes courage."
—Lao Tzu

"In combat one discovers there is no line between courage and vulnerability; one does not exist without the other."
—David Morehouse, PhD

We either have what we desire or the reasons why we don't. If your intention is to turn your reasons into results, you must believe in yourself more than you believe in your reasons. Once you honor what's in your heart and make courage your BFF, your reasons will no longer have any power over you.

7.8

As a result of growing up in the shadow of our survival instinct, most of us spend so much time trying to avoid looking like an ass that we never really know what it's like to put ours on the line.

What's more, whenever we choose to avoid anything at all, we rob ourselves of our vision, our aliveness, and our joy. No matter what you're committed to, unless you give up your fear of being judged, all you'll ever achieve will be governed by what you already know how to do without appearing foolish.

Fortunately, once you're willing to strap on your courage and put your butt out there, you'll be amazed at how quickly you put an end to the thievery.

> "To begin is the most important part of any
> quest, and by far the most courageous."
> —Plato

Courage isn't the absence of fear; it is the emotion that inspires you to override your mind when it's screaming at you not to.

7.9

Even in an uncertain world, the universe is always sending us everything we need to thrive. However, it's your job to sift through the drama in order to find it. Success, therefore, is a function of taking full advantage of everything that serves you while refusing to entertain anything that doesn't.

Mastery is for those who, as quick as they are to align with those on a similar path, they are even quicker to show any and all imposters the door.

> "Keep away from people who try to belittle your ambitions.
> Small people always do that, but the really great make
> you feel that you, too, can become great as well."
> —Mark Twain

Although the universe is forever sending us who and what we need, we must refuse to be distracted by anything that doesn't seem to fit. If it speaks and acts like an eagle, it's an eagle. If it doesn't, it's a turkey. Eagles soar above the drama. Turkeys—well, you know…

7.10

No matter how committed you are to a specific outcome, it's totally normal to have doubts when you're in pursuit of something grand. And, since it's also normal to think about giving up, it's extraordinary when you choose to keep going.

Therefore, if your intention is to be extraordinary rather than normal, I invite you to step beyond your comfort zone today and stay your course—even as your mind is begging you not to.

Remember, even when your little voice is filling your ear with second thoughts, whether you surrender to your doubts or listen to your heart is forever up to you. Listen wisely.

> "Fear is simply your mind trying to protect you, which must never be mistaken for it trying to help you."
> —Steve A. Becker

It's never what we're afraid of that prevents us from achieving what we want; it's an absence of courage and committed action. Fear shows up on its own. Determination is up to you.

7.11

Being happy and fulfilled has very little to do with what you're doing and everything to do with fully loving and appreciating the one who's doing it, which, of course, is you. Although we've all been taught to avoid blowing our own horns—for good reason—whenever we confuse humility with playing small, we're actually living a lie.

Energetically, playing big has nothing to do with ego—unless you allow it to—and honoring your ability to show up in all your glory is precisely why we are here. In fact, it will never serve you to leave your magnificence or your courage at home—nor will it serve you to shine your light solely on yourself.

Ultimately, playing full-out is a function of showing up versus showing off, which is why all the joy imaginable is for those who say no to their egos while saying yes to their passion.

> "To thine own self be true, and it must follow, as the night the day, thou canst not then be false to any man."
> —William Shakespeare

Be conscious of what you're leaving in your wake as you're creating it, and you'll be blessed with many more happy memories than regrets.

7.12

As addicted as we may be to procrastination, the surest way to overcome our aversion to doing anything we don't like doing is to intentionally step up and get it done.

Energetically, avoidance is a drug, so the only way to beat your addiction to it is to strap on your courage and simply do the thing you fear. Once you do, you'll realize that courage is an even stronger drug and even more addictive.

Ultimately, whether you're living your life addicted to excuses or to results is always up to you.

Choose your addiction wisely.

> "When you surpass the human state, your angelic nature will unfold
> beyond this 'existing world.' Surpass the angels then enter the Sea."
> —Rumi

Are you avoiding something or pursuing something grand? No matter what you're avoiding, it's robbing you of your aliveness. Results are for those who just say no to the thievery.

7.13

Has anyone ever advised you to not put too much pressure on yourself? If so, they may as well have suggested that you give up on your dreams. In fact, when it comes to manifesting your vision and making things happen, you can either live the rest of your life avoiding pressure or accept it as a sign that you're on the right track.

Energetically, momentum is a function of experiencing pressure as your partner rather than an adversary, which means interpreting it as a green light rather than a red light. In other words, pressure is your accelerator rather than your brake.

Ultimately, no matter how you're perceiving it, it's about refusing to overthink every little thing; allowing fear to be your signal to hit your *go* button (instead of your *off* button) and reinventing yourself as your own hero rather than someone who values comfort more than stepping beyond your comfort zone.

Would you prefer to have what you want—or all the reasons why you don't? At the end of the day, since the only way to create momentum is to choose courage over comfort, results are for those who make the right choice.

"No pressure, no diamonds."
—Thomas Carlyle

Being successful has very little to do with what you're pursuing and everything to do with fully honoring and appreciating the one who is engaged in the pursuit, which, of course, is you. Mastery is for those who declare themselves a force for good and are forever true to that. It's about who you are being and not who you're trying to become. Once you've chosen to show up as the hero you were born to be, there's no such thing as pressure.

7.14

One man follows a trail up a mountain and is inspired and grateful. Another is worried about getting lost, and as soon as he sees his first snake, he wonders what the hell he was thinking.

Although we are literally wired to be on the lookout for trouble, within each of us exists the ability to step beyond our wiring with an intention to lose ourselves in the inherent wonder of it all (as opposed to falling prey to our default inclination to be on the lookout for everything that could go wrong).

Ultimately, since it's literally impossible to put our instincts on hold, success is for those who refuse to dream smaller dreams—even as their minds are imploring them to do so.

Once you override your natural tendency to worry about every little thing with an intention to step beyond the ordinary, all the joy you can imagine will be yours.

> "If you are not willing to risk the unusual, you
> will have to settle for the ordinary."
> —Jim Rohn

Happiness is a function of accepting what is. Success is function of desiring more and refusing not to have it. Mastery is a function of knowing that life is a game and being grateful for every opportunity to play. Bliss is a function of igniting the fire in your heart and sharing your love and your light with the universe. If you want to wake up on fire, be the flame!

7.15

No matter what your little voice is imploring you not to do, it's forever within each of us to step beyond our considerations and fully into our power. In other words, we have every ability to bring our full intention to the party—even when our survival mind is pleading with us to let it run the show.

All of us tend to wonder if we have what it takes, but it's fully within you to override your primal fears in support of showing up as the capable and competent superhero you were born to be. It's not so much about waking up with a new insight where your doubts used to be; it's about stepping into your courage and beyond your fears.

> "Within you right now is the power to do things you never
> even dreamed possible. This power becomes available to
> you just as soon as you can change your beliefs."
> —Maxwell Maltz

Only by calling off the search for what you perceive to be missing will you discover that the only thing that's really missing is your ability to fully appreciate what isn't missing.

7.16

Whenever we set a new goal, as difficult as it may be to get started, momentum is for those who continue to take action even when their minds are saying no. In fact, as long as you continue taking action, every step you take actually stands on the shoulders of the preceding step, and each step gets progressively easier.

Even so, momentum must never be mistaken for results, which is why it will never serve you to put your feet up too soon. Ultimately, the greatest success is for those who keep running even after they cross the finish line.

> "Life is exactly what you dare to make it and Fortune favors the bold. So boldly step up and dare to make your life Magnificent."
> —Joseph McClendon III

Although it's been said that getting started is half the battle, getting started is simply a moral victory. In fact, people start things all the time only to give up as soon as the going gets tough. As clear as it is that staying the course is the real battle, it's actually the entire battle, which is why the surest path to success is for those for whom failure is not an option. Ultimately, if you truly intend to succeed, it's imperative that you fully own your outcome, find the lessons in every setback, and never give up.

7.17

As committed as you may be to a particular outcome, how often do you allow self-doubt to rob you of your intention? What gifts aren't you using? Where do you justify playing small?

No matter what you perceive to be standing between you and your dreams coming true, wouldn't you prefer to have what you want rather than the reasons why you don't?

Fortunately, no matter how much you believe in your reasons (limiting beliefs), once you start believing in yourself more than your reasons, your reasons will magically disappear.

Remember, it's fear that's stopping you, disguised as reasons, when all that's really lacking is courage. In reality, those things you've been calling reasons are simply your mind grasping at straws. Once you show it a little courage, the straws and your fears will quickly disappear.

> "If you bring forth what is within you, what you bring forth will save you. If you do not bring forth what is within you, what you do not bring forth will destroy you."
> —Jesus Christ

Although it's impossible to live a life that's free of making mistakes, it's fully possible to live a life that's free of repeating them. Mastery is for those who collect lessons and not regrets.

7.18

You can either have what you want or the reasons why you don't. In other words, if you truly want what you want to show up, you must believe in yourself more than you believe in your reasons. The only thing that ever holds any of us back is fear (disguised as reasons), yet all that's really missing is courage.

Once you unleash your courage—which is already within you—into the universe, all of your reasons will magically disappear.

> "It does not matter how slowly you go as long as you do not stop."
> —Confucius

If you are human, you were born with fear. Fortunately, you were also born with courage. Success is for those who honor their courage more than their fear.

7.19

No matter what you have been conditioned to believe, your power is in no way tied to the ebb and flow of forces beyond yourself. Still, might a major challenge slow you down or otherwise impede your progress in some way?

Perhaps—yet it's fully within each of us to remain focused on our ultimate destination in spite of any detours that show up when they do.

In every moment, whether you allow the winds of change to determine where you're heading or refuse to let anything blow you off course is totally up to you. No matter how windy it is, you are in charge of your sails.

"If you're brave enough to start, you're strong enough to finish."
—Gary Ryan Blair

The first step toward discovering who you are is to acknowledge that you've been hypnotized into accepting who you are not. Mastery is for those who refuse to accept anything other than the truth.

7.20

Once upon a time, there lived a young prince with a penchant for self-improvement, so he taught himself to swim in the castle swimming pool. He also dreamed of becoming a diver, but from the certainty of the water, the high diving board appeared to be very, very scary—so he never had the guts to give it a try.

Fortunately, it wasn't too long before his fairy godmother showed up to remind him that, from the certainty of his lounge chair, he once believed that the pool was just as scary!

The moral of the story? The path to achieving anything of value is sure to be paved with fear, and the only way to accomplish anything worthwhile is to get off your butt, strap on your courage, and go slay some dragons.

Although all of us were meant to live as kings and queens, the only way to avoid living life as a jester is to unleash your inner wizard. Once you do, as quickly as you can say bibble-dee-bobbity-boo, you'll instantly start "spinning your fears into gold" and be on your way to living happily ever after.

"Be guided by the hope of success, not the fear of failure."
—Robyn Benincasa

It's not the presence of fear that robs us of taking action; it's the absence of courage. Once you make courage your BFF and put an end to the thievery, you'll soon discover that you were meant to fly. Courage—never leave home without it.

Chapter 7 Key Concept

Honor your courage more than your fear and refuse to play small—even when your mind is telling you that you that you're neither good enough nor capable enough. First you bring the courage, then you get the results.

"Believe in yourself and all that you are. Know that there is something inside of you that is greater than any obstacle."
—Frank Clark

CHAPTER 8

Excellence and Playing Full-Out

Bringing All You've Got to All You Do!

What would it take for you to show up as a ten right now?

Where are you not willing to do so – and what would it look like if you were?

> "To play without passion is inexcusable."
> —Ludwig Van Beethoven

Mastery is for those who know that the secret to life is to replace doing just enough to get by with refusing to bring anything less than all you've got to everything you do. So, when would be a good time to leave playing small in the dust and replace it with playing full-out?

No matter what's vying for your attention, the key to showing up as the superstar you were meant to be is to remain true to *your intention* and totally ignore your little voice whenever it's begging you to re-think your plans rather than risk falling short.

In fact, because your mind was hoping you would make it all the way to the finish line without ever learning about his role as your door guard—including the fact that he's the one who's been whispering you're not good enough in your ear—it's no small accomplishment that you've made it this far.

You see, unless you've been reading these past few chapters with your eyes closed—and because you now know what you know about the five key elements—it's no surprise that your door guard is as resistant as he is to you also bringing *excellence* (element 6) and *playing full-out* (element 7) along for the ride. After all, imagine how worried he is about having to deal with you once you're dancing *like you mean it* with all seven elements.

And yet, there's really no reason to worry about him at all. For as resistant as he's been to you stepping into your power, as long as your intention is bigger than his resistance, he'll soon get the message that you're no longer okay with him running the show.

As you now know, although the five elements are the actual keys to bringing supreme certainty along for the ride, the actual delivery vehicle for bringing all five to the party is excellence. And since it's impossible for all five elements to deliver themselves, who do you suppose is already prequalified to strap themselves into the driver's seat, ensure that supreme certainty is riding shotgun, and bring every ounce of their passion with them wherever they go?

That's right. It's you. And since it's clearly you who's in charge of this process, the only thing that can ever thwart your intention is if you decide not to bring excellence to the party or decide not to play full-out.

However, because it's also up to you as to whether you're playing full-out and bringing excellence along for the ride, who do you suppose the excellence police should pull over if they see you bringing anything less than all you've got to the party? Well, first of all, you already are an officer with the EPD (the Excellence Police Department), so it's not that you simply need to start pulling yourself over more often—you need to stop letting yourself off with just a warning!

Seriously, why wouldn't you play full-out? For that matter, why would you ever leave home in the first place without your intention and purpose? And since you don't need any special training—remember that supreme certainty isn't a skill—the only other thing it will serve you to bring with you is your unwillingness to give up. Assuming, that is, that you are already bringing all seven elements along for the ride. But again, why wouldn't you?

In fact, now that you know that you're completely capable of accessing every ounce of your power at will, which includes knowing that there's no reason not to bring all seven elements to the party, I invite you to challenge yourself to continuously show up as the fully intentional game changer you were born to be.

Although all of us have it within us to show up this way, most of us rarely do. Why is that? Well, other than our natural inclination to play small, it's mostly because we rarely seem to care as much as we could, often believing that the more we care, the more disappointed we'll be should things not go our way—even though we really do care.

And since we do care more than we let on, whenever we commit to anything we truly care about—and then fall short for whatever reason—we're inclined to feel even worse than we did before we started caring. Then, even though our minds tend to perceive it as proof that we were actually wise not to care in the first place, all that really happened was that we fell into reaction to what occurred rather than refocusing our intention on learning from it and shifting back into our power.

Again, you likely did learn and shift back at some point, but it was only after enduring more pain than you would have if you had shifted sooner. To take it one step further, shifting actually is a function of caring; for if you didn't, why would you shift? In fact, whenever you truly care about something, you tend to be more passionate about it than you otherwise would be. Since we tend to care more once we're bringing our passion to the party than we do while waiting for it to show up, I invite you to replace waiting with caring—simply because you can.

Remember, whether excellence is the energy behind you playing full-out, or whether you're playing full-out because you're committed to excellence, mastery is for those who are willing to simply live in this question and be fully committed to never leaving home without all seven elements in tow.

Even so, unless and until you accept that you are the source of your own intention, your mind will never stop trying to prove to you that you're not, imploring you to put an end to this little foray of yours into mastery.

Whether you're listening to your heart or to your little voice is forever up to you. At the same time, never forget that all you really need to know is that all of us were put here with the ability to bring the full measure of our passion to everything we do, which includes refusing to listen to your mind when it's trying to convince you otherwise.

I invite you to finally let your mind know that you're no longer interested in playing small and allow the following teachings to shine a light on what's possible once you do.

Chapter 8 Teachings

8.1

Excellence is a function of living a life inspired by your vision rather than settling for one that's shaped by your history. If you're truly committed to greatness, you must be just as quick to banish "good enough" from your vocabulary as you are to making playing full-out your mantra.
Consciousness is a result of divorcing your past, marrying your dreams, and refusing to show up as anything other than a hole in the universe through which the Divine can work its magic.
All the joy imaginable is for those who do.

> "The meaning of life is to find your gift. The
> purpose of life is to give it away."
> —Pablo Picasso

> "This is the true joy in life—the being used for a purpose recognized by yourself as a mighty one; To be thoroughly used up before being tossed upon the scrap heap. The being a Force of nature instead of a feverish, selfish, little clot of ailments and grievances complaining that the world will not devote itself to making me happy. I am of the opinion that my life belongs to the entire community and it is my privilege to do for it all that I can. Life is no brief candle to me, but a sort of splendid torch, which I have hold of for the moment, and I want to make it burn as brightly as possible before passing it on to future generations."
> —George Bernard Shaw

Leaders strive for excellence and not approval. Mastery is for those who devote more energy to doing things well than they do to trying to prove to others how well they're doing.

8.2

Contrary to popular belief, passion is neither scarce nor elusive. Even though the universe is overflowing with love and light, the culture has conditioned us to be on the lookout for what's wrong, to lament what isn't working, and to withhold the full measure of our aliveness until others make the first move.

Fortunately, since it's fully within each of us to override this conditioning, joyfulness is for those who make peace with life's imperfections, who are fully aware that they are the source of their own light, and who are forever shining it as brightly as they can on everyone and everything.

All the joy imaginable is for those who do.

> "We are shaped by our thoughts; we become what we think. When the mind is pure, joy follows like a shadow that never leaves."
> —Buddha

Quality is never an accident, which is why it only shows up when you do everything you do to the very best of your ability. First, you create it, and then it creates you. Excellence is for those who never accept good enough from anyone—especially themselves.

8.3

Happiness has very little to do with what you're doing, and everything to do with how you're showing up. In fact, if you want to be happy, it will serve you to engage as fully as possible with everything you do and do it as awesomely as you can. On the other hand, if playing full-out isn't your thing, although you have every right to dabble—or settle for whatever shows up on its own—I promise you it won't be awesome.

"Anything worth doing, is worth doing awesomely." *
—Aristotle

* Okay, he may have said "worth doing well," but he surely meant awesomely.

By simply being conscious of what you're leaving in your wake as you're creating it, not only will you gain access to a fuller appreciation of "the now", but to a future in which your happy memories far outnumber your regrets.

8.4

Leaders are those who spend more time striving for excellence than waiting for approval, and even more time looking to make a difference than for evidence that they don't.

Although there's no connection at all between how we're feeling and our willingness to bring excellence to the party, if you're waiting until you "feel like it" before playing full, you'll likely be waiting a long damn time. Results are for those who replace waiting with "knowing" that everything they've been waiting for has been waiting for them to give up the wait. No matter what you've been avoiding or why you've been putting things off, the only thing it will ever serve you to put off is waiting itself.

"What matters is how quickly you do what your soul wants."
—Rumi

Confidence isn't a feeling you attain from beyond yourself, nor it is it going to magically appear once you accumulate enough proof. Energetically, *certainty* is already within you, waiting for you to rid yourself of all the reasons why you're not feeling it. First you step into your power and make things happen—and then you'll feel it.

8.5

No matter how committed you are to your dreams coming true, it will serve you to give up all "hope". Give it up, and then replace it with *faith*. In fact, hope is a drug, which is no less likely to rob you of your passion than to leave you addicted to someday.

Energetically, hope inspires waiting, while faith inspires action—so if you're expecting God to show up, you—and your faith—must show up first. Of course, since everyone knows that God only helps those who help themselves, the best way to help yourself is to continue to *make* things happen rather than simply hoping things work out.

If you want the universe to align with what you're doing, you must give it something to align with.

"Do or do not, there is no try."
—Yoda

"Sometimes we stare so long at a door that is closing,
that we see too late the one that is open."
—Alexander Graham Bell

If ever you find yourself waiting for what you want to find you, I invite you to give your off button a rest. In fact, since failure is all too often a result of putting up our feet too soon, success is for those who don't even own an off button.

8.6

Hoping to become wildly successful without really expecting it to happen is pretty much like going shopping without any money. At the end of the day, unless you're okay with spending the rest of your life window-shopping, it's never about what you're dreaming of; it's about what you know in your heart you deserve.

Success, therefore, is for those who are committed to bringing every ounce of their passion to everything they're pursuing, and then refusing to take their eyes off the prize until it actually shows up—just as expected!

"A "standard" is not something you attempt—
it is something you do—period."
—Madeleine Homan Blanchard

Raising your standards is a good thing, yet unless you also refuse to settle for less, you may earn lots of praise—but nothing you can expect to take to the bank.

8.7

Whether you're working behind the scenes—running the show for someone else—or have built your own business, your ability to have it all has very little to do with what you're pursuing and everything to do with how you're showing up while engaged in the pursuit.

Even so, and although success is a wonderful thing, if you focus solely on the pot of gold at the end of the rainbow, you'll rob yourself of extracting all the joy you can out of the rainbow itself.

Joyfulness, then, is for those who bring all they've got to the party and take full ownership of how they're showing up while they're bringing it. No matter how tempted you are at times to bring less, you must never withhold anything from the one who's in charge of your success, which, of course, is you.

"When you have the courage to take ownership of your own
wellbeing, you will begin to see the world differently. You will
live differently. You will become rooted by your own strength
and power in every situation. You are the hero you've been
waiting for. You are the hero the world has been waiting for."
—Evy Poumpouras

Wisdom is for those who bring passion along for the ride rather than hoping it shows up once they get where they're going.

8.8

Although both are worthy of our intention, excellence does not equal perfection. In fact, as is infinity, perfection is just as much of an illusion as it is unattainable. If you're unwilling to strive for anything other than perfection, you are clearly set up to lose. Just as you'll never arrive at infinity—neither will you ever achieve perfection.

Excellence, on the other hand, is a grand intention and a noble pursuit—and an energy that we have every ability to bring to the party, at will. However, there's no way to actually arrive at excellence, given that it's a practice and not a destination.

Mastery, therefore, is for those who replace the pursuit of perfection with the practice of excellence and refuse to settle for anything less.

> "The will to win, the desire to succeed, the urge to
> reach your full potential … These are all keys that
> will unlock to door to personal excellence."
> —Confucius

Although all of us are fully capable of practicing excellence, most of us avoid doing so in order to avoid the disappointment of falling short. And yet, since it would be no less disappointing to fall short while settling for good enough, I invite you to replace good enough with excellence.

8.9

The surest way to turn any dream into a nightmare is to assume that you're on the road to success, when in fact, you are glued firmly to the path of least resistance. Frankly, if ever you catch yourself looking for rest stops from the on-ramp, unless you're willing to rethink putting your feet up too soon, you have no right to expect your dreams to come true.

Success is for those who are clear about where they're going and why and who are committed to fording every stream, climbing every mountain, and knowing that there will be plenty of time to rest when they are no longer breathing.

"When lovers of life get ready to dance, the
earth shakes and the sky trembles."
—Rumi

Whenever you choose to take the easy way out, you rob yourself of your aliveness and your growth. No matter what life throws your way, by simply refusing to bring anything less than all you've got to everything you do, you'll instantly put an end to the thievery.

8.10

If it sounds too good to be true, it probably is. There are no hidden secrets or magic bullets (other than your own focus, dedication, and persistence). Will it serve you to seek the counsel of an acknowledged leader who knows of what they speak? Absolutely—for there is no reason to reinvent the wheel if you're able to learn from a respected guru who has clearly been there and done that. Even so, it will serve you even more to run as fast as you can from anyone who is trying to sell you a miracle cure or a surefire way to get rich quick.

At the end of the day, if you truly intend to succeed, you must be willing to invest an appropriate amount of time and money, surround yourself with superstars, and never give up.

"Excellence is to do a common thing in an uncommon way."
—Booker T. Washington

Although it's our fear of failure that causes most of us to give up too soon, it's giving up too soon that causes most of us to fail.

8.11

No matter how frustrating life can be at times, here's a little coaching: don't be a jerk! As an executive-level coach and consultant, I am privileged to have worked one-on-one with thousands of truly amazing people. I've also encountered those who have become so jaded that they've allowed their failures and limiting beliefs to justify their negativity. Although it's never their intention to be annoying, they've simply lost touch with their vision and compassion. For the most part, you should never go anywhere without checking your look in the mirror—and you mustn't forget to adjust your attitude as well.

> "Pay no attention to negative people. They
> have a problem for every solution."
> —Buddhist teaching

Honor and respect—don't leave home without them.

8.12

Success is for those who are perfectly clear about what they want and why they want it. In fact, once you refuse to settle for anything less than you deserve, you will realize that you are no longer distracted by every little thing that is vying for your attention. What's more, by finally stepping into your power, you will find that your fear of missing out and your inclination to get sucked into everyone else's drama have totally disappeared.
At the end of the day, living "in the flow" is really nothing other than honoring your intention to say yes to what serves you and no to everything else.

> "If your intention is to be happy and successful, look in the mirror,
> expecting to find the amazing and powerful person you are. See your
> potential, believe in it, knowing that as you believe it, you will not
> only emit that energy, but nothing can stop you from having it all."
> —Nathalie Botros

Excellence never shows up on its own. First you create it, and then it creates you. If you want to be successful, never accept good enough from anyone—especially yourself.

8.13

Expecting more out of life than you're willing to put into it is like hoping to win the lottery without buying a ticket. At the level of what's so, although we have very little control over whether we win or lose, we have total control over how we play the game. What's more, whatever shows up in return for what you're putting out there is a lot more likely to be something of value when value is what you're putting out there.
When quality is what you sow, quality is what you reap.

> "What if we were willing to ask ourselves, "If this was 100 percent right, what would I do differently?" Then do that. This is what transforms us from being ordinary into being extraordinary."
> —Faith Gorski

The universe always reflects back what you're sending it, so karma's only a bitch if you are. Send wisely.

8.14

No matter what you do for a living, you are either living the life of your dreams—or you're not.
In every moment, whether you're doing all you can to achieve your goals or still trying to figure things out, waiting for someday is neither a viable strategy for success nor a pathway to power. Therefore, even if you're unsure about your long-term goals, it will serve you to engage as fully as possible with whatever you're committed to making happen right now, with every intention of making it reality. After all, if it's worthy of your time and attention, it's worthy of giving it all you've got.
Mastery is for those who make excellence their default intention and know that no matter where they've been, all that really matters is the energy they bring to where they're going.

> "The secret of change is to focus all of your energy not on fighting the old, but on building the new."
> —Socrates

When you focus on what's lacking, you lose sight of who you truly are. Joyfulness is for those who spend more time celebrating what is than worrying about what isn't.

8.15

Each and every one of us is inherently whole and complete and magnificent beyond our wildest imaginations. And yet, if you sit around waiting for your magnificence to show up, the only thing you'll discover is that it didn't show up while you were sitting around waiting.

Joyfulness, therefore, is for those who have no interest at all in either waiting for someday or bringing anything less than every ounce of their passion to everything they do. In fact, although we all have reasons why we hold ourselves back, it's never our excuses that keep us small; it's our fear of what totally unleashed might look like.

At the end of the day, once you honor your magnificence more than your reasons, and your passion more than your fear, you will discover that unleashed is who you were always meant to be.

> "Not the sun or summer alone but every hour and
> season yields its tribute and delight."
> —Ralph Waldo Emerson

Passion is the natural state of the universe. "Toned down," therefore, is a reaction, which appears real only if you buy into it. Don't buy in.

8.16

If you truly intend to succeed, I invite you to give your off button a rest. In fact, success is a function of remaining fully engaged and on purpose—and since the first known ingredient in any recipe for disaster is putting your feet up too soon—why put your feet up at all?

For the most part, achieving what you want has very little to do with simply pursuing what you desire; it's about how you're showing up while you're engaged in the pursuit. Clearly, there will be plenty of time to play small when you're no longer breathing, so I invite you to put off playing small until then…

> "Excellence is not a gift, but a skill that takes practice.
> We do not act 'rightly' because we are excellent, in
> fact, we achieve excellence by acting rightly."
> —Plato

If you're not waking up on fire, it's because you're not going to bed with a purpose that's lighting you up. Even so, it's not so much about you "getting lit," it's about your intention to light up others.

8.17

Contrary to popular belief, *certainty* isn't a feeling you acquire from beyond yourself, and it isn't going to magically appear once you accumulate enough proof.

Certainty is an *intention* that we have every ability to bring to whatever we're doing simply because it's within us to do so. In other words, certainty is forever waiting for you to rid yourself of all the reasons why you're not feeling it in the first place.

Mastery, therefore, is for those who have called off the search for who they already are, and who bring certainty along for the ride simply because they can.

> "Self-mastery is knowing who you are and knowing who you are not."
> —Dawn Harlow

No matter how long you're willing to wait for your doubts and fears to go away, the only thing you'll discover is that they didn't go away while you were sitting around waiting. Certainty—don't leave home without it!

8.18

> A prospective student approached a martial arts teacher and said, "I am devoted to studying your system. How long will it take me to master it?"
>
> The teacher casually responded, "Ten years."
>
> The student said, "But I want to master it faster than that. I will work very hard. I will practice every day—ten or more hours a day if I have to. How long will it take then?'
>
> The teacher paused for a moment and replied, "Twenty years."
>
> —Zen teaching

Where in your life are you allowing impatience to gum up the works? Where are you more attached to alacrity than quality? Urgency can be a powerful motivator—but not when you value it above wisdom and excellence. Mastery is for those who put more energy into doing things well than they do to searching for a shortcut.

> "We are what we repeatedly do. Excellence,
> then, is not an act, but a habit."
> —Aristotle

Doing what you are expected to do is gratifying. Doing what you do to the absolute best of your ability is life altering. Are you living life—or is it living you? In every moment, we are either living or *being lived*. Happiness is for those who refuse to be the dust. Be the wind.

Chapter 8 Key Concept

You are the source of your own excellence. Once you commit to playing full-out, there's no reason to bring anything less than everything you've got to everything you do.

"He who tastes, knows."
—Sufi aphorism

CHAPTER 9

Gratitude and Abundance

Saying No to Scarcity!

What are you most grateful for right now?

If you were to bless three souls with an anonymous blessing today, who would they be and what would they be grateful for after they received it?

"Gratitude turns what we have into enough."
—Aesop

Mastery is for those who are aware that life is a game and are no more grateful for the games they win than they are for what they learn from the ones they don't.

For the most part, we are inclined to accept that whenever we're in the presence of anything deserving of our gratitude, a simple thank you is enough to adequately express our appreciation. Hence, the way that gratitude very often shows up in our lives is as little more than an auto-response. In other words, more of a reaction than an intention, which couldn't be further from the truth.

In fact, gratitude is the very essence of intention. It's the icing that we have every ability to apply to any cake we choose, and it's forever up to us what we're calling cake in the first place. On this side of knowing that you needn't listen to your survival mind, you are totally free to apply your icing (your gratitude) to anything and everything you decide to apply it to—simply because you can.

Since you already own this ability, once you fully embrace this truth, you will discover that the energy that allows you to bring the full measure of your passion along for the ride and inspires the universe to shower you with all the abundance you deserve is gratitude itself.

Gratitude, therefore, is always the clear and obvious choice, especially when your mind is trying to convince you that it's not.

Although it's impossible to be grateful when you're living in reaction, ironically, gratitude is the quickest way out of reaction. Even so, given that your survival mind is literally wired to focus on what's missing (scarcity), the only way to access the gratitude that's already in your heart is to intentionally bring it with you wherever you go. In fact, gratitude is not only your secret superpower, but the intention that allows you to override your scarcity mindset whenever your mind starts pointing out what you've yet to attain or accomplish.

Since your mind spends all its time focusing on what isn't, it will serve you to spend the next several minutes ignoring your mind and focusing on everything for which you are grateful. As you continue to allow gratitude to be the focus of your intention, I invite you to create an actual list of everything for which you are specifically grateful; starting with whatever comes to mind and including anything else you can think of as you're writing. Allow yourself to enjoy this process, ignoring your little voice when you hear it saying, "OK, that's enough."

As it implores you to stop writing, allow yourself to be grateful for your new awareness that you are not your little voice—and that you own the ability to ignore it and keep writing. At the same time, trust yourself enough to know that, at some point, you will intuitively know that you have achieved the result.

Of course, you may not see the value in pausing right now—perhaps thinking that you don't want to take the time—or you'd rather make a few mental notes instead. Clearly, it's up to you as to whether you create your list right now or wait until later but notice any resistance you may be having to doing so—while allowing yourself to be honest about what's behind this resistance. Once you're willing, I invite you to be empowered by completing this exercise…

Gratitude List and Abundance Exercise

1. What are you most grateful for right now?
   a. your relationships (significant other, family, friends, special individuals)
   b. your career and/or education
   c. your health and fitness
   d. your finances
   e. your lifestyle
   f. your psychology/level of mastery/willingness
2. Who do you need to thank for their support with regard to each item above?
   a. Create a list of these individuals, including a date by when you will reach out.
   b. Who are you most grateful for? Who contributed most to you being you?
3. What are you grateful for in advance?
   a. What actions must you take to begin to make these things real?
   b. What items on your Life Plan are you willing to focus on this week?
4. What are you grateful for having done for others?
   a. Who are you showing up for as a hero right now?
   b. Who else could use your support right now?
5. Who are you willing to let know how much you love and appreciate them?
   a. Create your list of who, and what you want them to know.
   b. When would now be a good time to let everyone know?

> "Dwell on the beauty of life. Watch the stars
> and see yourself running with them."
> —Marcus Aurelius

Ultimately, the ability to embrace gratitude and allow it to impact our relationships is a gift, and it serves us to give it to ourselves and others simply because we can. In fact, once you accept that *you* are the gift, you will realize there is nothing truly in the way of you being grateful in every moment. And once you accept that there's no reason not to be grateful, you will know in your heart that it's fully within you to become the giver of gratitude to everyone in your life, including yourself.

Gratitude isn't so much about what you have as it is about being grateful for being grateful, yet it certainly includes everything for which you are materially grateful (friends, achievements, events, and stuff) as the icing on your personal cake.

"Wear gratitude like a cloak, and it will feed every corner of your life."
—Rumi

No matter how much gratitude and icing you may have baked into your personal cake, abundance is a function of knowing that it's not so much about what you want, it's about what you fully intend to *cause* to show up in general. In other words, it's a function of intentionally walking around with the five key elements in one hand and a can of icing in the other, willfully bringing excellence along for the ride and playing full-out.

However, because abundance is both an intention and a state of mind, it's also about taking ownership of how you ultimately intend to show up in every moment, including taking responsibility for how much gratitude you're bringing to the party, as well as your willingness to show up as the creator of the destiny you deserve and have every right to expect.

Although you do need to take action to claim what the universe is holding in escrow with your name on it, there is nothing you need to acquire from beyond yourself to justify that you are worthy or deserving of doing so. Again, since everything you need is already within you, you have absolutely nothing to prove and every right to expect it.

Ultimately, it's about manifesting your destiny from a mindset of *knowing* that it's already a done deal. And although you may have a sense this is true, you must be willing to give up the belief that scarcity is somehow ingrained in your psychology. When, in fact, scarcity is simply a limiting belief that exists solely because we grew up in an environment that gave birth to this way of thinking.

In actuality, the only reason we continue to fall prey to a scarcity mindset is because we're inclined to believe that if we were to embrace the belief that we deserve it all, we'd have to let go of our belief that we don't. When, in fact, we simply need to *stop* thinking small and *start* thinking big. Therefore, it's critical that you give up the belief that you're stuck in scarcity and replace it with *a knowing* that you are no less abundant or deserving than anyone else.

Ultimately, since unlocking the door to abundance and gratitude is simply a matter of doing so, when do you suppose would be a good time for you to start thinking big? Clearly, the answer is now—but only after you surrender to the fact that the universe never responds to who you think you are, it responds to who you *believe* you are.

As you accept and believe that you have it within you to think big, it's critical that you put those bigger thoughts into action and then wrap them in gratitude as you set them free. In support of this intention, I invite you to allow the following teachings to shine a light on what's possible once you do.

"Being grateful. That's the first step on the path to joy."
—Sarah Ban Breathnach

Chapter 9 Teachings

9.1

Miracles abound, but even if you're expecting one to show up, unless you're consistently bringing something worthy of a miracle to the party, you can wait until the cows come home—and all you'll get is cows.

Energetically, no matter how confident you are that you're deserving of a miracle, it will never serve you to focus on what you feel you deserve, but on what you're putting out there.

And yet, no matter what you're putting out there, only by shining your light as brightly as you can on everyone else will the universe be inclined to send you a miracle—which includes those things that initially show up as challenges—for although we rarely appreciate them for what they are, our greatest challenges are often our greatest teachers.

Mastery, then, is for those who are as quick to see the lesson in every challenge as they are to see the miracle in every lesson.

No matter what you think you deserve, gratitude is for those who are quicker to count miracles than challenges, and just as quick to count their blessings.

> "The one who was always in my thoughts, for whom I've searched so long, has come to me with open arms, laying flowers on my path."
> —Rumi

Wisdom is for those who are not only willing to question what they think, but where they are thinking it from. Once you are willing to see beyond the illusion that your random thoughts are of your own creation, the truth will set you free.

9.2

There is nothing at all un-spiritual about the pursuit of all the material wealth you both desire and deserve. In fact, living in alignment with one's natural state of abundance is the ultimate expression of the human spirit. However, what does matter is whether gratitude is the energy behind what you're doing (in alignment with your intention to contribute and make a difference) or if your ego has taken over and is simply showing off.

Although we have very little control over what we receive, we have total control over what we're putting out there, including its quality, its value, and how grateful we are for the ability to do so.

> "What a precious privilege it is to be alive—
> to breathe, to think, to enjoy, to love."
> —Marcus Aurelius

Abundance is a result of being fully aware that you and your possessions are temporary. Whether your journey through life is a spirit-quest or an ego trip has everything to do with whether you focus more on what you have or on sharing who you are. Miracles are for those who share.

9.3

Unless you're willing to take the time to visualize your dreams coming true, why would they?

In fact, envisioning yourself having the things you desire is the energetic equivalent of planting the seed of your intention within the garden of the universe. If you fail to cultivate that seed with action and water it with gratitude, your dreams will likely remain just that—dreams.

Therefore, it you truly want those dreams to come true, I invite you to step beyond simply hoping things work out by bringing both your gratitude and your watering can with you everywhere you go.

Desire + Clarity + Action + Faith + Gratitude = Whatever Your Heart Desires

> "The key to a successful life is waking up every
> day with an attitude of gratitude."
> —Frank Clark

If having a breakthrough was easy, it wouldn't be a breakthrough. Therefore, if you truly intend to have one, instead of looking for a way around your fears, make gratitude your BFF, show up as the hero you were born to be, and refuse to take your eyes off the prize until it shows up.

9.4

Even as the universe is calling your name, how are you responding? Are you envisioning and pursuing all that you desire or waiting to be inspired? Inspiration is for those who have no desire to wait—who take full advantage of everything the universe is sending in their direction—and who accept that if they ever put their intention on hold, they'll likely be waiting forever.

By being grateful in advance for all that you desire—while also taking action in support of it showing up—inspiration will find you! At which point, by simply continuing to take action as the universe/God shines a light on your path, all that you refuse to live without will be yours.

"Gratitude is not only the greatest of virtues, but the parent of all others."
—Cicero

Although the law of abundance is always in play, it's up to you to have faith, embrace what shows up, and be open to figuring out how it serves you. Only by giving up on having to have things *your way* will you be able to see the magic in every little thing.

9.5

If ever you're feeling down, it will serve you to reflect upon all that you've accomplished (versus contemplating all the things you haven't) and celebrate everything for which you are grateful. If you recall something for which you're not grateful, be grateful you survived it, then let it go. Gratitude is a function of spending more time appreciating what is than lamenting what isn't. Although it's perfectly normal for all of us to question certain things about our pasts, it will never serve you to question your ability to soar like the eagle you were born to be.

"You have no cause for anything other than gratitude and joy."
—Buddha

Mastery is for those who are willing to question what they think *and* where they are thinking from. Once you say no to scarcity and yes to abundance, where you're thinking *from* will no longer be an issue.

9.6

As a result of being raised under the cultural influence of a scarcity mindset, which is tied to our inherent fear of not being deserving enough, most of us tend to worry about losing what we have and missing out in general. Unfortunately, when we allow the fear of loss to run our lives, it prevents us from planting any new seeds and being fully open to what's next.

Energetically, unless you're actually expecting something of value to come knocking on your door, there's no reason for it to do so—and even if it did, you'd be inclined to turn it away.

Mastery is for those who expect the universe to send them what they need, are grateful for it in advance, and are forever planting seeds in favor of it showing up.

No matter what your conditioning is whispering in your ear, abundance is for those who say no to scarcity and yes to everything else.

> "Reflect upon your present blessings, of which every man has plenty, not on your past misfortunes, of which all men have some."
> —Charles Dickens

Are you pursuing all that you deserve or waiting for clarity? Clarity has nothing to do with waiting and everything to do with taking action. Once you're moving forward with courage and conviction, clarity will find you.

9.7

Joyfulness is for those who are quick to focus on all that's right in their world and even quicker to override their default inclination to be on the lookout for what's wrong. Whenever you allow yourself to be distracted by what you perceive to be missing—or why you believe you don't have it—the universe is obliged to align with your scarcity-driven considerations. However, once you redirect your energy and your focus to everything for which you are grateful and refuse to settle for anything less than you deserve, the universe will reward your intention instead. Remember that what you see is what you get.

> "Appreciation is a wonderful thing. It makes what is excellent in others, belong to us as well."
> —Voltaire

Abundance is for those who have made peace with life's imperfections and know that no matter what they've yet to accomplish, they are never more than one win away from the edge of glory.

9.8

It's been said that variety is the spice of life, but our very pursuit of anything new and different tends to rob us of our appreciation for what we already have. In fact, *gratitude* is the spice of life, for in its absence, even our greatest accomplishments tend to show up as mundane.
At the end of the day, there is absolutely no joy in taking life for granted. Therefore, if you want to be happy, I invite you to take pause, count your blessings (rather than your challenges), and shake a little gratitude on every little thing the universe sends your way.

> "Don't wait for someone else to bring you passion. You already are the passion you are putting out there. Generously share your love openly and you will invariably receive love and passion in return."
> —Dr. Erika Schwartz

Passion is for those who bring gratitude along for the ride rather than hoping it shows up once whatever they've been waiting for shows up at their door.

9.9

If you're ever feeling stuck or off purpose, notice where you've been making yourself or others wrong—and then be willing to simply let it go. No matter how you're feeling, your feelings are nothing more than proof that you are human—so it will serve you to honor your intention and gratitude long before you honor how you feel.
Once you take ownership of your humanity and are willing to replace your knee-jerk reactions with empathy and your doubts with faith, all that you'll feel from that moment on is unstoppable.

"We can only be said to be alive in those moments
when our hearts are conscious of our treasures."
—Thornton Wilder

Abundance is a function of bringing intention and gratitude along for the ride rather than waiting to see how we feel once the ride is over. First, you show up with the gratitude, and then the universe shows up with the abundance.

9.10

Joyfulness is for those who spend more time counting their blessings than they do worrying about what's missing. In fact, although worrying tends to age us, celebrating who we are and sharing our gratitude with the universe is pretty much like hanging out at the fountain of youth.

Therefore, if remaining youthful is more appealing to you than counting new wrinkles, I invite you to put *counting your blessings* at the top of your to-do list.

"Do not spoil what you have by desiring what you have not; remember that what you now have was once among the things you only hoped for."
—Epicurus

You are in control of how much gratitude you bring to the party in any given moment. Whether you spend your time counting challenges or blessings is always up to you. Count wisely.

"My day begins and ends with gratitude and joy."
—Louse Hay

152

Chapter 9 Key Concept

You are in control of how grateful you are—not your mind. Even in upsetting times, it's fully within you to be certain of your value instead of worrying about what's lacking. If ever you find yourself dancing with scarcity, refuse to allow it to take the lead.

"Everything comes to you in the right moment. Be patient. Be grateful."
—Buddha

Section III Exercises
Turning Passion into Action

You are the designer of your life. Discovering that it's fully within your power to create the life of your dreams by overriding anything that's preventing you from doing so.

1. Know that it's fully within your power to choose to play big every day. What, if anything, is preventing you from doing so?

    What have you been afraid of? Where are you no longer willing to let fear stop you?

    What would playing big look like for you? What specifically would you do right now?

2. What dreams have you had that you've been too afraid to even write down?

    Where have you not been playing full-out—and how do you intend to change that?

3. Review your gratitude list (from chapter 9) every day for the next seven days, then as often as it serves you moving forward. If you have not yet created your list, please do so now:

Expanded Gratitude List / Abundance Exercise

1. What are you most grateful for right now?
    a. your relationships (significant other, family, friends, special individuals)
    b. your career and/or education
    c. your health and fitness
    d. your finances
    e. your lifestyle
    f. your psychology/level of mastery/willingness to take ownership

2. Who do you need to thank for their support?
   a. Create a list of these individuals, including a date by when you will reach out.
   b. Who are you most grateful for? Who has contributed most to you being you?
3. What are you willing to be grateful for in advance?
4. What plans or actions must you take to begin to make these things real?
5. What items on your Life Plan are you willing to focus on this week?
6. What are you grateful for having done for others?
7. Who are you showing up for as a hero right now?
8. Who else could use your support?
9. Who, right now, are you willing to let know how much you love and appreciate them?

Complete your list of these individuals and what you want them to know.

When would now be a good time to make that first call?

SECTION IV

The Art of Living on Purpose

By the end of this section, you will be unwilling to create anything other than fully conscious and ever-expanding relationships with everyone in your life, including yourself and the universe.

VII.   Love and Relationships Loving Full-Out
VIII. Synchronicity; Harnessing the power of Coincidence
IX.   A Force for Good; Showing up as the Loving Leader you were Born to be

Exercises: Turning Love and Intention into Action
You are responsible for the quality of your relationships! It's fully up to you to take ownership of how you are showing up in every moment.

CHAPTER 10

Love and Relationships

Loving Full-Out!

Who are you willing to reach out to and bless with the sound of your voice with your heart in it?

Whose day is about to be brighter because of you? Why not do so right now?

> "We don't find extraordinary relationships, we *create* them."
> —Traci Porterfield

No matter with whom you are speaking, mastery is for those who refuse to let anything other than love do their talking. Although all of our relationships are deserving of our full attention, unless you bring your full *intention* to creating the love relationship of your dreams, you'll likely end up with nightmares down the road.

Truth 1: Relationships are where all the magic happens—
but only when you own yourself as the magician.

Truth 2: Since you're the one with the magic wand, it's up
to you to make your partner's doubts disappear.

Truth 3: Unless you embrace and apply all that you've learned in chapters 1–9, the magic wand won't help.

It's critical that you know what you want out of a relationship, but it's even more important to be clear about what you intend to bring to it. Specifically, the level of your devotion & compassion, as well as your willingness to embrace the following four secrets and nineteen teachings.

"The Four Secrets to Creating and Celebrating a Fully Conscious and Loving Relationship"

1. The first secret to creating an extraordinary relationship is to actually "make it your thing."

Declare your commitment to it. Focus on it. Water it. Nurture it. And above all, own it. Since most of us are aware of what it feels like to break up with someone, we're inclined to resist opening our hearts as fully as we can when we meet someone new, withholding the full measure of our devotion "just in case." However, this actually tends to have a reverse effect on the likelihood of things working out since whenever one person withholds their full intention, it inspires the other to withhold theirs as well, which pretty much ensures that anything that may have begun to blossom will eventually wither on the vine.

The Fix:
A. Knowing that it's entirely possible to be both prudent and *all-in* at the same time.
B. Hold nothing back. Be in it to win it.
C. Go first. Live and love on purpose. Open your heart and play full-out!

2. The second secret is to fully own and override your cultural conditioning.

For women, this tends to show up as being distrustful of men, which men perceive as being reserved. For men, it's an inclination to show up as less than fully respectful of the feminine, which women can't help but notice since it feeds their distrust even further. Many men aren't even aware that they are showing up this way—primarily because it's so deeply ingrained and typically more subtle than overt (yet not as subtle as women wish it was).

The Fix: Give up waiting for a cultural revolution. Although an entire book could be written about why these dynamics exist, the more immediate solution lives in our willingness to allow for the fact that they do exist and counter them by intentionally overriding our inclination to react from our conditioning with a commitment to fully honor and respect each other instead. Joyfulness is for those who bring both an open mind and an open heart to every interaction.

3. The third secret is to be willing to let go of your history—then actually do so!

Intend to put an end to living in reaction to anything you've been allowing to exist as issues between you and your partner. Although you can never make any hurtful memories disappear, you're fully capable of letting go of the meaning you've attached to those memories.

All the joy imaginable is for those who willfully redirect their focus to what they intend to create moving forward versus focusing any energy on where they've been or what they've been through. If you spend all your time looking in your rearview mirror, you will ultimately find yourself somewhere other than where you want to be.

The Fix: No matter who's done what to whom, even as you're willing to own your role in the matter, it will never serve you to get caught up in who was to blame or to continue to allow your past to influence your present or your future in any way. Passion is for those who focus on what *is* and not on what *was*.

Tip: Revisit the *forgiveness process* in chapter 4.

4. The fourth secret is to override your ego by living and loving on purpose.

Although this is pretty much the secret to life in general, when it comes to creating a magical relationship, it's imperative that you put your ego on the shelf and intentionally show up as the gift you truly are to each other—as well as who you promise to be forever. Remember:

A. We have full control over how we show up and what we give.

B. We have zero control over what we get.

C. There is no C.

The Fix: No matter what's going on elsewhere in your life, it's critical that you fully honor your intention to put your partner first. In fact, once you're making it about them—and they are making it about you—the only thing that can ever prevent your relationship from being a recipe for pure magic is if one of you forgets the recipe, so here's a little coaching: Don't forget the recipe!

Ultimately, it's always about what each of you are bringing to the relationship. It's not about keeping score. If only one of you is bringing while the other is taking, this is out of alignment with the recipe for pure magic. It's a recipe for disaster. So, if you'd rather create magic than a disaster, shine all your light on each other—and never stop doing so. I invite you to allow the following teachings to shine a light on what's possible when you do.

Chapter 10 Teachings

10.1

Are you currently experiencing all the love you deserve or waiting for it to find you? In matters of the heart, you'll find others a lot more open to you making a withdrawal if you first honor them with a deposit. If all of us were waiting for others to make the first move, who would go first? I invite you to go first.

> "How can you ever hope to know the Beloved
> without becoming in every cell the Lover?"
> —Rumi

You wouldn't withhold water from a flower until it blossoms—so why withhold your love until you feel it's deserved? Love first—and then enjoy what blossoms.

10.2

Although all of us have been conditioned to believe that it's important for us to continuously work on keeping our love alive, if you want a magical relationship, you must immediately stop working on it and create it instead. Once you and your partner give yourselves the gift of falling madly in love with each other each and every day, you'll realize that there's nothing to work on. Remember, love isn't a thing that magically shows up on its own; it's both an intention and a promise, which you have every ability to consciously bring forth as you continue to give it away.

"Now join your hands, and with your hands your hearts."
—William Shakespeare

Although most of us are inclined to wait until our partners do something deserving before we treat them in a special way, if you treat them special first, you won't have to wait so long.

10.3

The experience we have come to know as love has nothing at all to do with acquiring a feeling you don't already have from somewhere beyond your own creation. Love is who you are.
In fact, whenever you do open your heart and share yourself fully with others, you will know it as the most authentic expression of your intention. Otherwise, whenever you're not allowing your love to flow freely, you're actually withholding your truth. And when you withhold your truth, you're lying. In which case, here's a little coaching: Don't be a liar. Be a lover.

"Every heart sings a song, incomplete, until another heart whispers back. Those who wish to sing, always find a song."
—Plato

All the joy in the world is for those who bring love along for the ride instead of hoping it shows up once they get where they're going. Once you know that love is who you are, that's pretty much all you really need to know.

10.4

Whether the bridge to your heart is cluttered with conditions or open and inviting is always up to you. There is no legitimate way for any of us to declare our love to be unconditional at times and then conditional when it serves us. Within the realm of what's so, we are either loving unconditionally or we're not, and when we're not, it's because we're living in reaction to our own preconceived rules and beliefs (in other words, our conditions).

Ultimately, if unconditional love is something you intend to share unconditionally, you must first get rid of the clutter.

"Love is the bridge between you and everything."
—Rumi

Withholding your love until you feel it's deserved is like reserving your best china for special occasions. Once you accept that *you* are in control of how you apply your conditions, you'll find that the secret to making every occasion special is you.

10.5

Loving unconditionally has very little to do with what's flowing out of you and everything to do with what's flowing *through* you. By aligning with *that* which gave rise to the universe, you become one with the primal forces of love (pure feminine) and intention (pure masculine), and you will know in your heart that you are never alone. However, when you allow your ego to have its way, you are effectively trading all that is infinite for whatever your survival mind is serving up in that particular moment.

In every moment, whether what you're sharing with the rest of us is your love and your light or a piece of your mind is entirely up to you. I invite you to share what's in your heart.

> "Those who bring sunshine to the lives of others
> cannot keep it from themselves."
> —Sir James Barrie

We were created to live in the glory of our true selves as vessels through which the Divine can work its magic. All the joy imaginable is for those who choose to be vessels.

10.6

Each and every one of us is pure love, waiting to happen. For that reason, nowhere in your life will it serve you to play small or otherwise diminish your light in order avoid outshining others. Instead, what will serve you is to shine your light as brightly as you can and never stop doing so.
In fact, since sharing your love and your light with others is the highest form of service, if ever you're not sharing it, you're aiming pretty low. I invite you to aim higher.

> "Love is of all the passions the strongest, for it attacks
> simultaneously the head, the heart, and the senses."
> —Lao Tzu

You are the light; you simply forgot. You are the power, yet sometimes you're scared. Although we've all been conditioned to believe that suffering is a result of circumstances beyond our control, suffering is actually a function of withholding your love and your compassion. Stop withholding.

10.7

The universe adores you and is totally aligned with your grandest, most heartfelt intentions. As for being enamored with your ego? Not so much.

When you're living with intention and in alignment with the greater good, it will shine a light on your path and show up as your partner in sending you all you need.

However, if you've chosen to make your life about "win or lose" or "right or wrong" or are otherwise striving for dominance at the expense of others, be prepared to go it alone.

> "On this path let the heart be your guide".
> —Rumi

Disappointment is a result of letting yourself or others down. Passion is the result of doing the right thing and doing it as often as you possibly can. Therefore, whether you're feeling passionate or disappointed is always a matter of intention. Intend wisely.

10.8

If you ever feel lost or off purpose, allow yourself to be renewed by the reflection of joy from the faces of those you bless with acts of kindness. No matter how poorly we may feel at times, the pathway back to inner peace is paved with service, so you may want to keep your eyes peeled for any opportunity to do a little paving.

Once you're open to seeing them, you'll notice plenty of deserving souls who could use your support. At which point, even if your own circumstances have caused you to forget that *you* are the gift, the surest way to be reminded of this truth is to reach out and be one.

> "Happiness is a choice and smiles are free."
> —Aaron Gryder

> "The greatest compliment that was ever paid to me was when someone asked me what I thought and attended to my answer."
> —Henry David Thoreau

Happiness is for those who replace waking up wondering what the day is going to bring with waking up already knowing what they are going to bring to the day.

10.9

What part of your partner are you trying to tame? No matter how often you feel the urge to rein in someone's strengths, it will serve you to step beyond your ego's need to outshine others, and then inspire them to shine their own light as brightly as they can in support of your mutual outcomes. Although being a leader is a privilege, you'll never have any followers if you fail to honor and empower those you are leading to be leaders themselves. Once you surround yourself with superstars and allow them to excel at what they do, you'll be blown away by what you're able to accomplish together.

> "The heart of a fool is in his mouth, but the
> mouth of a wise man is in his heart."
> —Benjamin Franklin

Rule #1: It's not about you.
Rule #2: Never forget rule #1.
The Lone Ranger had Tonto, who would have never stuck around if he didn't feel appreciated. If there's someone in your life who it will serve you to thank, reach out to them right now—and *two* lives will soon be a little brighter.

10.10

Living in a state of unconditional love must never be mistaken for unconditional acceptance. Just because you have a loving heart, it doesn't mean that you're willing to look the other way when someone shows up in your space with something other than an honorable intention. In fact, it's entirely possible to care deeply for others while still denying anyone access to your inner circle unless they are willing to play nice in the sandbox.

An unwillingness to spend time with anyone who's okay with letting themselves or others down has nothing to do with being judgmental; it's about refusing to compromise your intention and your standards.

Withholding your approval doesn't mean you're withholding your truth; it means you're simply saying no to something that you're unwilling to endorse.

> "We are shaped by our thoughts; we become what we think. When the mind is pure, joy follows like a shadow that never leaves."
> —Buddha

Whenever we choose to look the other way, we rob ourselves of our integrity and our aliveness. Only by refusing to compromise either your integrity or your standards will you ultimately put an end to the thievery.

10.11

Sadly, too many of us spend more time complaining about what's wrong with our relationships than we do nurturing and celebrating them. If you devote more time to thinking about breaking up than you do to working things out, what do you suppose is more likely to happen?

Taking each other for granted is certainly not a strategy for everlasting love, but neither is waiting for your partner to make the first move. Relationship bliss is for partners who appreciate and celebrate all they've created together by watering each other daily. Regrets are for those who settle for going it alone. Why settle?

> "'Tis better to have loved and lost than never to have loved at all."
> —Alfred Lord Tennyson

The moment you start listening to your ego instead of your partner, you have no right to expect anything more of tomorrow than to wake up yet another day older—and without a partner.

10.12

The quality of our relationships is in direct proportion to how much honor and respect we have for one another. An entire chapter could be written on this topic alone, but by simply allowing love to be the author of everything that's flowing out of your mouth, you'll never have to say, "I'm sorry."

It's never really about what we're saying, it's about what's *behind* what we're saying. That is why you must never say, "I hear you" unless you're really listening. Only by giving others the gift of truly hearing what they have to say will you be given the gift of being heard.

> "The very center of your heart is where life begins.
> The most beautiful place on earth."
> —Rumi

Men, there are two theories with respect to arguing with women. Unfortunately, neither one works. Therefore, if you want a magical relationship with a woman, you must play by the rules:

Rule 1. She's right.
Rule 2. She's always right.
Rule 3. Listening to each other fixes everything.

10.13

In any given moment, we are either living on purpose or *in reaction* to our fear of not being good enough. Therefore, whenever we meet anyone for the first time, the ego takes over and compels us to pretend to be someone we are not.

Unfortunately, since this dynamic almost always kicks in when we first start dating someone, given that our imposter is now interacting with their imposter, it's only a matter of time before we tend to wonder how real it all is. In fact, since most of us have become so adept at putting our imposters out there, it's only natural for us to question whether we're enamored with whomever we think we're dating or if we're falling in love with their disguise.

Ultimately, no matter how brilliant your own disguise may be, if true love is your outcome, I invite you to leave your costume hanging in the closet where it belongs.

"To love or have loved is enough. There is no other
pearl to be found in the dark folds of life."
—Victor Hugo

Wherever you go today, I invite you to leave your ego at home, override any inclination to prove anything to anyone, and intuitively speak from your heart. Give the universe the gift of *you* today—not your disguise.

10.14

Even though the culture has conditioned us to believe that love only shows up when it does, it's fully within each of us to share our love unconditionally—even when others remain stuck in their conditioning. Instead of withholding your love until you feel it's deserved, know that you are fully capable of opening your heart and shining your love on others simply because it's within you to do so.

"Being deeply loved by someone gives you strength,
while loving someone deeply gives you courage."
—Lao Tzu

Joyfulness is for those who are forever shining their light on others, whether they feel it's warranted or not. If you're ever wondering if your love is warranted, I invite you to know that it's always warranted—whether you feel it's deserved or not.

10.15

You needn't go searching for a place to play when the world is your playground. Nor must you wait for love to show up when you know in your heart that love is who you are. Joyfulness is not only for those who bring their passion with them wherever they go; they share their love unconditionally simply because they can.

There are many things to consider when it comes to deciding who you are going to spend the rest of your life with, but why withhold your love and your light from the rest of us until you do? In every moment, you are in control of how much passion you're willing to bring to the party. Why not bring it all?

"Don't wait for yet another lover to sweep you off your feet. Find beauty and passion in every moment of your life with gratitude and kindness, and then watch your lover become everything you've been searching for."
—Dr. Erika Schwartz

Love is simply a concept unless it's shared. You have full control over how much love you feel by creating it as you give it away. Waiting for love to show up will get you nothing but older.

10.16

Love is a function of communication. Even when we disagree, we need to *get* each other. Over time, within the normal ebb and flow of any relationship, all of us have said and done things that have caused our partner to feel pain—even though we didn't intend to hurt them. Failing to take responsibility for having done so is akin to ignoring the eight-hundred-pound gorilla in the middle of the room. Therefore, to reignite our passion, we must give up our reasoning that any upset we caused was unintentional—even if that's true—then own what happened and apologize.

Only by replacing the gorilla with a heartfelt intention is it possible to access our ability to fall in love with each other every single day—*forever!*

"Being someone's first love may be great, but to be their last love is beyond perfect."
—Anonymous

It's never about what we get; it's about what we give away. It's never about how appreciated we feel; it's about how much we appreciate others. It's always what happens *over there* that matters.

10.17

Although all of us have been brainwashed into believing that it takes two to tango, it's forever within you to show up as the choreographer of your own relationship, choosing to remain true to your heart instead of allowing your ego to do your dancing for you. In every moment, it's fully within your power to override your mind's need to be right by intentionally stepping beyond it and replacing your natural inclination to react with a loving intention to show up as the loving partner you were born to be.

No matter what your little voice is whispering in your ear, it's always your call as to whether you think and act on purpose or surrender to your ego's inclination to control the situation.

When we interact with each other with an appreciation for the fact that love is who we are, we gain access to the love that is already flowing through us. Once your thoughts are shaped by love, the only thing you'll ever feel the need to control is your intention to shower it on your partner.

"Love is an irresistible desire to be irresistibly desired."
—Robert Frost

Ego is an imposter who is pretending to be you. Once you replace caring about what you are with sharing who you are, love will show the imposter the door.

10.18

If your intention is to create a magical relationship, you must immediately replace wondering "what's in it for me" with giving it all you've got. Relationship bliss is for those who are committed to saying no to their egos and continuously reinventing themselves as givers rather than scorekeepers.

Once you step beyond your ego's need to keep track of what's flowing in your direction and dedicate yourself to fulfilling your partner's needs before your own, you'll realize that you already have everything you could ever want.

> "When you like a flower, you pluck it. When you love a flower,
> you water it daily. He who understands this, understands life."
> —Buddha

If you're hanging around waiting for passion to show up, you'll likely be waiting forever. What if everyone was waiting? First you do the watering, and then you get the flower.

10.19

The quality of our lives is the quality of our relationships, and the quality of our relationships is the quality of our communication. Quality communication is a function of listening with the intent to understand (rather than judge) and speaking with the intent to empower (rather than dominate or control). Wisdom is for those who are no less willing to embrace this truth than they are to make it their mantra—and are even quicker to put it into practice.

At the end of the day, if your intention is to create the relationship of your dreams, it will serve you to listen to your own heart *and* to every little thing your partner has to say.

> "Our sweetest experiences of affection are meant to point us to
> that realm, which is the real and endless home of the heart."
> —Henry Ward Beecher

Whether you're allowing your voice to serve as a loudspeaker for your ego or as a messenger of your heart is always up to you. Once you allow compassion and respect to be the authors of everything that's flowing out of your mouth, you'll never have to say, I'm sorry.

"Don't count on someone else to make you happy or complete. Do the work to make yourself happy. Although it can be exceptionally difficult, frustrating, and confusing, it is absolutely necessary. Make a commitment to yourself first. Your partner will thank you for it."
—Traci Porterfield

Chapter 10 Key Concepts

Be first with giving love. Withholding love is withholding your truth. What you bring to the relationship is what you are destined to receive in return. Relationships are not meant to be worked on; they are meant to be created.

"You, yourself, as much as anybody in the universe, deserve your love and affection."
—Buddha

CHAPTER 11

Synchronicity

Harnessing the Power of Coincidence

Celebrating what you desire in advance of it showing up is the energetic equivalent of planting a seed for that very thing within the garden of the universe!

Step 1: Create a list of what you want the universe to send your way, including how each item on your list aligns with your personal vision, and also serves the greater good.

Step 2: Next to each item, declare how you intend to show up in order deserve and attract it.

Step 3: Be aware that you may not always get what you want, but you will get what you need.

There are only two ways of looking at things. One way is to be on the lookout for what's possible. The other is to be looking for reasons why it's not. Wisdom is for those who, instead of lowering their expectations to avoid feeling bad if things don't work out, have raised them to avoid missing out when the bird of paradise shows up with an actual delivery.

When was the last time something happened to you purely by chance, and because of that random coincidence, you were either made aware of something you felt might serve you in a meaningful way or you met someone you felt you needed to get to know even better? And, in the wake of being inspired to do so, you made a conscious decision to follow through—so you did!

Even though you had a feeling that these random coincidences might lead to something special, it was stepping up and doing what you needed to do that ultimately led to you taking advantage of them to the degree that you ultimately did, which wouldn't have been the case had you not said *yes*.

Of course, it's just as likely that you can recall a similarly random situation where a similarly random opportunity appeared to be no less promising, but it would have required you to step so far beyond your comfort zone that it was far easier to decline the universe's invitation than it was for you to say yes—so that was what you did. You allowed your mind to make your decision for you by telling the universe, "No, thanks. I'm good."

Obviously, you don't have access to a time machine and can't travel back to the moment when you chose to say no to that invitation, but if you were able to go back, change your answer to yes, and return to here and now—how might your life have turned out? What if you had not taken a pass on whatever the universe was sending in your direction? There's no way of knowing for sure, but given how often saying yes has otherwise served you in the past, why would you not make saying "yes" your default response from now on?

As potentially rewarding as it may be to say yes rather than no, the real power of synchronicity is for those who are actively looking to take advantage of specific opportunities, keeping their radar on and their eyes open for anything and everything flowing in their direction. Specifically, opportunities that would have likely been dismissed as simple coincidences in the past, but where you're now willing to dance with everything that shows up and follow those breadcrumbs until you discover what the universe has up its sleeve…

Of course, since there's no way of knowing how things would have turned out had you not avoided calling that certain person or put off making that certain decision, I invite you to look in the opposite direction and reflect upon a situation that's clearly working for you right now— questioning if it would it be working if you hadn't met one or more specific people you now call friends or said yes to a coincidence that is now serving you in a positive way?

Think back to how you met that individual and the role that synchronicity (serendipity) clearly played in you doing so. Was it a last-minute change in plans, saying yes to an invitation you normally wouldn't have, or some other unforeseen circumstance that resulted in you being somewhere you wouldn't have been otherwise? A situation where you wouldn't have met that person—and wouldn't be doing what you're doing now—if not for that coincidence? Maybe you didn't consider it a coincidence back then, having simply considered it *good luck* or being in the right place at the right time.

No matter what you call it, synchronicity is *always* in play—and is very likely the source of just about everything fortuitous that has ever landed on your doorstep or otherwise injected itself into your life in a meaningful way. In fact, many of those things may have initially shown up as something you perceived as *bad* luck—crappy weather, heavy traffic, a postponed flight, or any similar inconvenience or change in plans that may have resulted in you being late, ending up somewhere else, or otherwise finding your way into a specific circumstance where you wouldn't have otherwise ended up—if it wasn't for whatever appeared back then to have happened by chance. But was it?

Although the universe is always intervening on your behalf, there are two specific factors that tend to determine the level at which you are inclined to take advantage of synchronicity (AKA, the Law of Attraction); both of which are tied to whether you're showing up *in reaction* to whatever the universe is sending your way or choosing to go with the flow and dance with the situation on purpose:

1. Noticing that you would have had to say yes to both an initial coincidence as well as to whatever showed up in response to that initial *yes*. Otherwise, it would simply be showing up in your life right now as something to which you said *no* (a missed opportunity).
2. Being aware of the level at which you are willing to continue to say yes to everything that you're now able to recognize and identify as synchronicity.

After all, why wouldn't you? For even when you engage with anything in anticipation of what you foresee as possible, it's always up to you to decide how long you continue to do so and where you allow it to lead you.

At the end of the day, synchronicity is always a result of the universe shining its light on your path and then leaving it totally up to you to choose to say yes or no. On behalf of the universe, I invite you to say yes.

In celebration of everything that may already be in escrow waiting for you say yes, the following teachings will allow you to shine a light on what's possible when you do.

"What you seek is seeking you."
—Rumi

Chapter 11 Teachings

11.1

Whether we are conscious of it or not, everything that any of us might ever find useful is forever flowing in our direction. Unfortunately, unless we see the immediate value in whatever lands on our doorstep, too many of us are inclined to turn it away.

Frankly, the universe knows what it's doing, which is why it will serve you to entertain everything that shows up with a more open and receptive energy. What will serve you even more is to let karma do its thing.

Once you give up the need to have things your way and are willing to embrace what the universe is sending your way instead, you may just find that it's precisely what you've been waiting for.

"When you let go of the ego self, what you are
getting in exchange, is the whole universe."
—Adyashanti

Life is a treasure hunt, but only by surrendering to the notion that you have no clue what you're hunting for will you ultimately be able to see the treasure in every little thing.

11.2

Envisioning yourself living the life of your dreams without planting any seeds within the garden of the universe is like digging a bunch of holes in your yard, hoping to find a treasure you never buried. In other words, unless you let the universe in on what you want and are consistently acting like you deserve it, you can keep hoping until hell freezes over—and all you'll get is a really cold place to spend eternity.

Obviously, you would never wait at the pickup window at a drive-through without placing an order first—so unless you're actively planting seeds and watering them daily, you'll likely be waiting a long damn time. On the other hand, once you put your desires on loudspeaker and begin moving in that direction, even after the universe starts sending you what you need, it'll want to know, "Would you like some fries with that?"

> "Believe you deserve it, and the universe will serve it."
> —Unknown

Although the law of attraction is always in play—and everything in your life is showing up for a reason—it's still up to you to make sense of it all and have faith. Magic is for those who do.

11.3

Change is inevitable, and although it's inherently disruptive, it's very often the means by which you are delivered the missing pieces to your puzzle. In fact, whether you're conscious of it or not, the universe is forever sending you everything you need. Even so, if you focus more on what got disrupted than you do on what's possible, you'll spend the rest of your life lamenting every little thing that didn't go your way.

Destiny is for those who see the silver lining in every setback, are inspired by every hurdle they've had to overcome, and are eternally grateful for how much they've grown as a result.

> "Change is never painful, only your resistance to change is painful."
> —Zen proverb

Anyone can lower a bar in order to feel good about clearing it. Even so, success is never about how high you need to jump to get over it, but "who you need to become" in order to do so.

11.4

The path to anywhere worth going is bound to be cluttered with obstacles. We can either bitch and complain about them or embrace them and dance with them on our way to the promised land, which is a matter of perceiving them as lessons rather than regrets.

Once you give up resisting the things that appear to be standing in your way and are willing to go with the flow, you will naturally and intuitively overcome any and all obstacles in your path.

In nature, no matter how large a rock might be, water simply flows around it—no trying required. Don't be the rock. Be the water.

> "What you think, you become. What you feel, you
> attract. What you imagine, you create."
> —Buddha

It's impossible for the universe to fill anything other than a receptive vessel. If you simply observe nature, you will see this is true. Therefore, unless you give up having to have things your way, you'll continue to miss out on what it's sending you. If you truly want what you want to show up, be receptive.

11.5

Even if we're not aware that it's happening, the universe is forever sending us the missing pieces to our puzzle.

Even so, no matter how receptive you feel you are in allowing it to do so, the fact that most of us believe that we already have a pretty good grasp on reality tends to impede our ability to be open to anything that shows up beyond the realm of what we believe to be possible.

Energetically, since it's impossible for the universe to fill a vessel that's already full, unless you're willing to give up having to have things your way, you'll continue to miss out on what it's sending. True wisdom, therefore, is for those who accept that no matter how much they know, they don't know it all.

"Synchronicity: A meaningful coincidence of two or more events where something other than the probability of chance is involved."
—Carl Jung

Faith isn't the absence of doubt; it's the energy that allows you to override your mind when it's screaming at you not to. Abundance is for those who trust the universe more than they trust their minds.

11.6

Are you actively pursuing all that the universe is holding in escrow with your name on it?

Or, are you waiting for clarity? Frankly, unless you're already taking action in pursuit of what you want, you are sending a message to the universe that you're expecting *it* to make the first move—which is like waiting for something to be delivered that you haven't ordered yet.

Unless and until you put your dreams on loudspeaker, the universe will have no clue what to send in your direction—and you'll likely be waiting forever.

Energetically, there's no way for anything you desire to show up unless you're living on purpose and have absolute faith that you'll be sent the missing pieces to your puzzle. First you take the leap, and then the universe will shine a light on your path.

"All that we are is the result of what we have thought. If a man speaks or acts with an evil thought, pain follows him. If a man speaks or acts with a pure thought, happiness follows him, like shadow that never leaves."
—Buddha

What are you expecting to show up today? Are you open to having something magical happen? Are you waiting for the other shoe to drop? It's never too late to shift your expectations.

11.7

Mindfulness is a function of replacing the mindless pursuit of the next shiny object with the intentional doing of whatever it takes to achieve what you really want.

Success is for those who are just as quick to align with their vision and their purpose, as they are to identify what they need to do next—which is almost always a matter of simply trusting the universe to shine a light on whatever that might be.

Even so, only by being willing to give up having to have things your way will you discover that everything you need is already flowing in your direction. Magic is for those who let it in.

> "As painful as it may be, a significant emotional event
> can be the catalyst for choosing a direction that serves
> us more effectively. Look for the learning."
> —Louisa May Alcott

Being needful of something tends to make it about the lack of it, which causes us to focus on what's missing. Abundance is for those who focus on what's present and not on what isn't.

11.8

Although most of us would like to succeed in a grand way, very few of us are really expecting it to happen. Unless you're able to imagine yourself attaining more than a reasonable level of success, that's likely all you'll ever achieve.

Since you already own the ability to break free from your scarcity mindset and the confines of your self-imposed box, simply shift your focus to what you actually want—as well as why you want it—envision it as already a done deal and continue to take action until it shows up.

Doing the same thing over and over again while expecting a different result is the definition of insanity; it's also why so many of us tend to remain stuck where we are. Success, therefore, is for those who are no longer thinking from inside the insanity box because they've smashed it to smithereens.

"Once you make a decision, the universe conspires to make it happen."
—Ralph Waldo Emerson

If you don't really expect your dreams to come true, you will be inclined to settle for less—and less is exactly what the universe will be sending you, if and when it does.

11.9

Certainty is a function of knowing that you already know everything you really need to know. Wisdom is knowing that you don't know it all. Faith is a function of expecting the universe to send you what you need and knowing that you may not even be aware of what you need until it shows up.

The law of attraction is always in play, but unless you're open to what you want showing up on its terms—even as it comes knocking at your door—you'll be inclined to turn it away. The first thing you need to know is that the universe knows what it's doing—so everything it's sending you, it's sending you for a reason.

All of us have access to the same field of gold, but destiny is for those who know they are seeing what they were meant to see, and they will intuitively do with it what they were meant to do.

"It's not what you're looking at that matters, it's what you see."
—Henry David Thoreau

Only by letting go of the need to have things "your way" (otherwise known as control) will you be able to see the magic in every little thing. So, might today be the perfect time to do so?

11.10

The more you fail to take advantage of all the coincidences and serendipities the universe is sending in your direction, the more they will continue to live as missed opportunities and regrets.

Whenever you disregard a coincidence with your name on it, you are robbing yourself of what's possible in the moment and your ability to attract whatever else you need in support of manifesting the life you were meant to be living.

The sooner you stop walking around with blinders on and start paying attention to all the magic that's flowing in your direction, the sooner you'll put an end to the thievery.

> "The mind that perceives the limitation is the limitation."
> —Buddha

Continuing to ignore all of the coincidences that "just happen to show up" in your life is akin to telling the universe, "No, thanks. I'm good." Frankly, the universe has been around a lot longer than you have, so it will serve you to say *yes* whenever serendipity knocks on your door and invites you to let it in.

11.11

The universe is forever sending us the missing pieces to our puzzles, yet most of us fail to take the hint. Are you willfully taking advantage of all the serendipities flowing in your direction (no matter how subtle) or waiting for clarity? Frankly, waiting for more clarity before acting on a coincidence is like waiting for an investment to pay off before you're willing to buy in. Clarity is for those who trust their intuition, replace waiting with embracing, and then immediately begin to make sense of anything that shows up. Only by giving your heart to the universe and allowing it to shine its light on your path will everything you've ever wanted start flowing in your direction.

"Your vision will become clear only when you can look into your own heart. Who looks outside, dreams; who looks inside, awakens."
—Carl Jung

If you sit around waiting for your dreams to come true, the only thing you'll discover is that they didn't come true while you were sitting around waiting. Once you replace hoping with expecting and bring gratitude along for the ride, all that you've been waiting for will find you.

"Vision without execution is delusion."
—Thomas Edison

Chapter 11 Key Concept

Until you let go of things having to go your way (control), you will miss the opportunities being sent your way—since they will rarely look how you think they should look. Remain open, have faith, and expect the universe to send you what you need

"The birds always find their way to their nests. The river always finds its way to the ocean."
—Zen Proverb

CHAPTER 12

A Force for Good

Showing Up as the Loving Leader
You Were Born to Be

How to Be a Force for Good-

1. Be a human being.
2. Be on the lookout for situations where you can make a difference.
3. Do whatever it takes to do so.
4. Repeat.

> "A hero is no braver than an ordinary man,
> but he is brave five minutes longer."
> —Ralph Waldo Emerson

Although most of us would likely reply, "Of course" when asked about our willingness to show up for others as a loving leader and a force for good, since so many of us are inclined not to show up this way as often as we could, why don't we?

Cleary, it's fully within our hearts to embrace our inner hero in support of those who could use our help, yet because things are a lot less likely to go wrong if we're able to make it to the end of the day without having to deal with anyone else's drama, it's simply easier for us not to. After all, not only are their problems part of their own circus—they're not our monkeys!

Given everything you now know about mastery, unless you're willing to settle for simply *understanding* all you've learned over the last eleven chapters (otherwise known as the booby prize), what will actually serve you is to take full ownership of everything you now know and immediately put it into practice.

In support of which, the *first* step in showing up as the loving leader you were born to be is to fully embrace the truth that is already flowing through you! Including the fact that you are *not* your mind, letting go of your past and your limiting beliefs, living in full alignment with your vision and purpose, and forever honoring your courage, your gratitude, and your magnificent intention to show up as a force for good! None of which has anything to do with showing off—and everything to do with showing up!

As inspiring as it is to finally take ownership of who you truly are, the *second* step to showing up this way is to actually bring the full measure of your intention to everything you do! In other words, being unwilling to simply hope that what you want is enough to steer you in the right direction, while bringing all you've got along for the ride in support of manifesting all you need on the way to making your vision a reality.

Even though the very essence of *showing up* is bringing your full warrior energy to the party—while being unwilling to show up as anything less than a hero—it also includes knowing that the power of playing full-out can be compromised in certain situations unless it's married to *loving* full-out as well.

All of us embody both masculine and feminine energies. Therefore, no matter how committed you are to showing up as a force for good and a hero (your masculine energies), in the absence of bringing both your *lover* and *magician* along for the ride (your feminine energies), your intention to be of service may be diminished to the degree that those you are supporting perceive where you're coming from as *rescuing* them rather than inspiring them to rescue themselves. In other words, making it a little too much about *you* than it is about them.

Of course, since mastery is very much about our relationships, the *third* step in showing up as the superhero you truly are, is to fully embrace your inner magician while allowing it to provide you with a more empowering way of showing up than you may have previously considered effective. In other words, you are allowing yourself to be open to anything you're able to download from the universe, which you likely wouldn't have had access to if you had simply remained reliant on your warrior energy—devoid of your feminine intuition.

Finally, the *fourth* step to showing up as the shining star you were meant to be is the willingness to dance with your masculine and feminine energies; knowing that since the *master key* to mastery is love, if you ever find yourself fumbling with the lock, love is your personal locksmith that always saves the day.

Still, in support of you actually showing up this way, although it's never about paying any less attention to your warrior or your magician, it is about wrapping everything you say and do in as much empathy and respect as possible before putting it within listening distance of those with whom you intend to make a difference.

At the end of the day, showing up as a force for good is the shining of your light as brilliantly as you can on everyone and everything the universe is sending in your direction. In other words, it's as much about honoring your innate ability to fully embrace who you were put here to be as it is about refusing to bring anything less than your full intention with you wherever you go.

In celebration of it all, we invite you to allow the following teachings to shine a light on what's possible once you dedicate yourself to mastering the art of living on purpose!

Namaste

Chapter 12 Teachings

12.1

Nothing of consequence has ever been attained by way of talent alone. In fact, given that pure intention has boldness and passion strapped to its back, no matter how skillful any of us may be, mastery is for those who know that the only thing that matters between the moment they declare an intention and the moment they achieve it is the moment they refuse to give up.

Vision + Love + Courage + Persistence = Anything Your Heart Desires

"Everything is hard before it is easy."
—Goethe

Each and every one of us was born with the ability to bring our full intention to the party. Whether you allow fear to limit your challenges or step up and challenge your limits is forever up to you. Success is for those who refuse to bring anything less than all they've got to everything they do—and then can't wait to do it again tomorrow.

12.2

"Pressure is a privilege."
—Billie Jean King

Being successful has very little to do with what you're pursuing and everything to do with fully honoring and appreciating the one who is engaged in the pursuit, which, of course, is you.
Leaders show up as a force for good. It is never less than a privilege for them to do so—even in the face of any pressure they may be under with regard to whatever it is they're pursuing.
Mastery, then, has everything to do with how you're being rather than who you're trying to be. By showing up as the leader you were born to be, you will find that there's no such thing as pressure.
It's never the obstacles in your path that keep you from staying your course; it's what you're telling yourself about those obstacles. Results are for those who are quicker to override the mind than succumb to anything they once perceived as pressure.

12.3

Destiny is never a matter of fate; it's a function of embracing what serves you and letting go of what doesn't. In other words, it's a matter of choice. Still, only by surrendering to anything that appears to have been chosen for you will you be granted access to alternative options, which typically lie hidden beyond the illusion that you have no other options.

Success is for those who've made peace with the past, have their eyes on the prize, and are willing to dance with everything the universe sends their way. Do all these things, with all your heart, and you will awaken every day knowing that you are in the right place.

> "One meets their destiny often on the road they take to avoid it."
> —French proverb

Leaders are those who are as quick to *forgive and forget* as they are grateful in advance for everything they're expecting to show up—especially once they've forgiven and forgotten…

12.4

Nothing is forever. Therefore, there's no reason to focus on anything you're afraid of or the fear of losing what you have. For at some point, all that you have will lose you.

Wisdom, then, is for those who fully appreciate things for what they are, absent of any need to own or control them, which is actually nothing other than a willingness to embrace the truth of who you really are.

No matter what's vying for your attention, the only things it will ever truly serve you to focus on are gratitude, faith, and your willingness to be amazed.

> "Respond to every call that ignites your spirit."
> —Rumi

There are many things in life that will grab your attention, but only a few that will grab your heart. Follow the ones that grab your heart.

12.5

When you let go of your dreams, you die. And yet, even if you have a dream, if you're simply waiting for it to come true, all you will ever achieve is the realization that it didn't come true while you were sitting around waiting.

Fortunately, by willfully embracing who you truly are, declaring yourself a force for good, and then bringing the full measure of your intention to everything you do, all your dreams will find you.

Desire + Intention + Decisive Action = the Life of Your Dreams

> "Respect yourself, and others will respect you."
> —Confucius

In the wake of any situation where you've lost sight of your dreams, reclaiming your power is a function of refocusing on what's possible rather than worrying about what isn't. No matter your history, mastery is for those who replace lamenting where they've been with celebrating where they're going.

12.6

If ever you feel like you've forgotten who you are, the surest way to step back into your power is to instantly override your natural inclination to feel sorry for yourself by immediately reaching out and supporting someone who may be suffering as well.

No matter how often or how deeply you fall prey to the fear of not being good enough, by simply shifting your focus back to making a difference—and then getting lost in your pursuit of that—your love and your light will instantly fill the space where any darkness used to be.

> "If your actions inspire others to dream more, learn more,
> do more, and become more, you are a leader."
> —John Quincy Adams

In every moment, whether you are shining your light on others as a force for good or living in the shadow of fear and doubt is always up to you. Although challenges are a part of life, suffering is optional. In fact, since none of us would ever suffer on purpose, suffering can only show up when you're not living on purpose. I invite you to live on purpose.

12.7

The greatest success is for those who are willing to knock down the door to their dreams while others are still fumbling with the lock. "Living the dream" is never a result of simply applying what you know; it's a function of how you're showing up while applying what you know.
Mastery is a function of refusing to embrace anything that simply speaks to your head unless it also speaks to your heart—and then following your heart all the way to the promised land.

> "What lies behind us and what lies before us are tiny
> matters compared to what lies within us."
> —Ralph Waldo Emerson

If you want an amazing life, be an amazing person. If ever you're not satisfied with what the universe is sending in your direction, upgrade what you're sending it.

12.8

Living into your vision from a higher state of consciousness has nothing to do with acquiring a level of knowing from somewhere beyond yourself. Consciousness is a function of honoring *that* which is already flowing through you—even as your survival mind is doing its best to convince you that no such thing exists. Therefore, your ongoing ability to show up in a beautiful state is forever dependent upon your ongoing intention to pay absolutely no attention at all to your little voice.

Once you refuse to listen to anything your mind has to say, commit to living your life on purpose, and dedicate yourself to being a force for good, the universe will shine a light on your path.

> "The door to higher consciousness can only be
> opened by the hand of the true self."
> —Erica Nitti Becker

> "Mastering others is strength. Mastering yourself is true power."
> —Lao Tzu

All the joy in the universe is for those who are committed to living in service of the greater good.
Mastery is for those who replace walking around in search of what's missing with an intention to make as much of a difference as possible while simply walking around.
Heaven is for those who do.

Chapter 12 Key Concept

Understanding is the booby prize. Refuse to show up to any situation with anything other than your greatness in tow. This is living your best life!

> "As long as you live, keep learning how to live."
> —Seneca

Section IV Exercises
Turning Love and Intention into Action

You are responsible for the quality of your relationships! It's fully up to you to take ownership of how you are showing up in every moment.

1. How aligned are you right now with the four secrets to celebrating and creating a conscious relationship? What can you do right now to make things better?
2. Where are you waiting for others to show you that they are committed before you commit to them?
3. Where are you withholding your love while waiting for another to go first?
4. Identify your cultural conditioning. In what ways are you looking for your man or woman to prove they can't be trusted?
5. What lessons have you learned from your bad relationships? How willing are you to simply let those memories go and move on? What must you let go of in order to do so?
6. With regard to excellence and playing full-out, what is preventing you from doing so?
7. When would now be a good time to shine your love and your light on everyone?
8. On a scale of 1–10, how open are you to having things happen by chance?
9. What have you achieved in your life by way of coincidence?
10. When did something unfortunate happen to you that later turned out for the better?
11. What do you really want? What is in the way of you achieving it—and what are you going to do about that?
12. Make a list of how you will celebrate when you achieve it.

AFTERWORD BY
ERICA NITTI BECKER

Congratulations! Your journey into mastery has come down to one final question. In the light of what you now know, what are you going to do next? Specifically, in what ways do you see yourself making the most of your new authentic voice?

Now that you are fully aware of your ability to live on purpose and are no longer compelled to listen to your mind, you are totally free to allow your authentic voice to be the inspiration behind every action you choose to take.

Still, even though your authentic voice is finally set free, since it is your mind's job to continue to plant seeds of doubt, it wouldn't be unusual at all for you to think, *I probably need to read all this again before I really understand it. I wonder how long it will be before I actually feel confident enough to put all this into practice.*

In fact, it would be more unusual for you not to be having these thoughts. So, when they do show up, know that this is normal, and then listen instead to your true voice—the one that has finally been awakened by everything you now know—the one that will forever be reminding you that you were put here to shine your light as brightly as you can on everyone and everything. This is the voice that wants you to know the answers to the questions about your purpose and why you are here. These answers will only become clear after you are actually living on purpose.

First you plant the seeds—and then you get the fruit. Once you are no longer asking yourself questions from fear and are asking them from intention, you will discover that you are a whole lot happier with the answers. Mastery is for those who ask the right questions.

To find your purpose, live on purpose.

Final Inspiration

We honor you for joining us on this journey and for trusting us with your most sacred resource: time. Although you may have been hoping for a step-by-step action plan that would teach you *how* to put everything you've learned into action, that would likely result in you simply living in reaction to what your mind would want you to do (which would just as likely be nothing). Instead, we are offering you something that will serve you a whole lot more.

This book is your resource. Live each day on purpose, taking full ownership of your intentional voice. When in fear, be courageous. When in doubt, be certain. When feeling overwhelmed, refer to the appropriate chapters with an intention to reclaim your purpose. Remember, you will still fall into reaction when you do. The *solution* is to know that you are human, step beyond it, and show up as the loving leader you were put here to be. When it's too dark for you to see with your eyes, use the light that is in your heart to choose your path.

Living the Philosophies of Chapters 1–12

Begin by reviewing all the exercises from the previous chapters, and then commit to living them. Keep track and decide how to reward yourself.

A. Put it all together! Ultimately, create your own thirty-day challenge; Make a list of what you're committed to doing on purpose for the next 30 days—and then do it.
B. Keep track of your wins—including your most incredible examples of successfully shifting from reaction to intention.
C. Do not keep track of your losses. Simply commit to turning them into wins—and then do so!

Namaste

www.distinctionsofmastery.com

Regarding Social Media

All of the individually numbered teachings included in this book are formatted in a manner to allow each individual teaching to be shared on social media, as long as each teaching is posted in its entirety and credited to: Michael Nitti / "Mastery: The Art of Living on Purpose." All other quotations are part of the public domain, yet should be credited to the author.

Contributors

Dr. Erika Schwartz: www.eshealth.com
Madeleine Homan Blanchard: www.kenblanchard.com
Aaron Gryder: www.aarongryder.com
Dawn Harlow: http://dawnharlow.com
David Morehouse, PhD: www.davidmorehouse.com
Evy Poumpouras: www.evypoumpouras.com
Joseph McClendon III: www.josephmcclendon.com
Loren Lahav: www.lorenlahav.com
Niurka: www.niurkainc.com
Nancy Pentilla Lemire: www.innermiracles.com
Claudette Anderson: www.claudetteanderson.com
Nathalie Botros: www.thebon-vivantgirl.com
Michelle Sorro: www.michelle-sorro.com
Traci Porterfield: www.traciporterfield.com

ABOUT THE AUTHORS

Erica Nitti Becker

Erica's philosophies of life are anything is possible and facing fear is your true teacher.

After surviving a near-death experience when she was thirteen years old, she experienced her first spiritual awakening. Doctors called her recovery a miracle. Through training both her brain and body back to health, Erica's thirst for life and her mission were sparked.

Through travel and adventure, she thrives on finding new adventures and experiences that require her to push herself through her fears and comfort zone in order to grow physically and spiritually.

Erica's defining moments have been skydiving over the Hawaiian Islands, competing in a twenty-four-hour, hundred-mile, multisport race through the desert, trekking more than forty miles in two days through the Grand Canyon (for Project Athena, a nonprofit organization), hiking Machu Picchu, and experiencing a kundalini awakening in Italy.

Erica has spent the past sixteen years—and the better part of her professional career—working for the most honored and respected life and business strategist, helping people achieve peak performance. For nearly a decade, she has been coaching business owners and professionals to enable them to achieve success on their own terms, professionally and personally. She has also consulted to many authors, speakers, athletes, and experts in a variety of fields.

Erica is passionate about teaching people how to master their minds, break through inner resistance, and bring awareness to living at a higher level of consciousness. Her spiritual beliefs and practices, in conjunction with her strong will, are a solid foundation for her insatiable desire to help people align with their purpose and passions. Her energy, passion, and enthusiasm are contagious to everyone around her.

Erica has passionately logged more than ten thousand one-on-one coaching hours, working with hundreds of clients. Her clients achieve the results they desire, and they also receive what they didn't know they needed.

Erica lives in San Diego, California, with her husband, Steve, and their rescue cat, Mad Max. Her passions are hiking, meditating, reading, writing, shamanic journeying, traveling, and having deep, transformative soul conversations with friends over a glass of wine.

www.ericanittibecker.com
Instagram: successcoacherica
Facebook: EricaNittiBecker

Michael Nitti

Michael has been touching people's lives, as well as their hearts, for more than four decades. As a full-time coach for more than fifteen years, Michael has worked with thousands of clients throughout the world, drawing upon all he has learned over thirty-five years of intensive transformational coursework and what showed up as a result of his spiritual awakening in 1983; after which, he continued working as a business professional while coaching and teaching on the side.

Having held executive-level positions in several industries, Michael found his true calling in 1997, when, thanks to his business expertise and his level of influence within the self-help industry, he was recruited by Robbins Research in San Diego. For the next eight years, he was privileged to serve as a member of Tony Robbins's executive team, which allowed him to travel the world in support of Robbins's extraordinary events and evolve his coaching skills while working directly for Tony. He served as a vice president for Robbins Research before transitioning into full-time coaching in 2005.

Since then, Michael has been one of the most prolific life coaches on the planet, coaching sixty to more than one hundred clients per month, which allowed him to refine and perfect his signature teaching, "The Trophy

Effect", which was published in 2009. That led him to being featured on the EXTRA television series *The Masters* in 2017. Having retired from Robbins in 2020, Michael continues to coach and consult privately with a focus on higher consciousness, unconditional love, relationships, and supreme certainty. Michael resides in Florida with his amazing wife of thirty years, Julie, and their darling little yorkies.

Facebook: Michael Nitti / IntentionQuest
Instagram: coachnitti
www.intentionquest.com
The Trophy Effect, Balboa Press and Amazon.com